Frida

Frida

Chosen to Die: Destined to Live

Frida Umuhoza Gashumba

With Sandy Waldron

Sovereign World

Sovereign World Ltd
PO Box 784
Ellel
Lancaster LA1 9DA
England

ISBN 978 1 85240 475 8

The publishers aim to produce books which will help to extend and build up the Kingdom of God. We do not necessarily agree with every view expressed by the authors, or with every interpretation of Scripture expressed. We expect readers to make their own judgment in the light of their understanding of God's Word and in an attitude of Christian love and fellowship.

Cover design by David Lund Design
Typeset by CRB Associates, Reepham, Norfolk
Printed in Malta

From my heart, I dedicate this book to . . .

Steven, my husband, who has believed in me so much
and encouraged me, even when I didn't believe in myself:
his love has made life sweet again;
every man and woman who had
a chance to live again after the genocide;
all our future generations, who are our children,
our heritage and hope;
my lovely children, Maxwell and Natasha;
my cousins, Adeline and Clarisse;
all my friends, especially Julienne for her support, prayer
and love in all the difficult and good times we had together;
to Aunt Anita for all her loving kindness and support;
to Martin Butarama for all his support and encouragement;
and to Constance and Stephan Funck for their constant
friendship, help and support.

And to the memory of:
my Grandpa and Grandma,
my Mama and Papa,
my brother César Uwineza (Kiki),
my sister Solange Umugwaneza (Mimi),
my brother Alestide Munyabugingo,
my baby brother Régis Dominique Shumbusho
and baby sister Gatesi Bénédicte.

May your souls rest in peace.

CONTENTS

Publisher's Foreword

This is the story of a remarkable woman who at the young age of fourteen found herself in the grip of one of history's most appalling atrocities – the 1994 Rwandan genocide. History books list the statistics of those that perished over a period of one hundred days, the death toll estimated by the United Nations to be 800,000.

Retelling the events here in this book Frida exposes mankind's frail humanity, illustrating how statistics merely feed impersonal impressions of the horror. Instead the genocide must be interpreted from the inside, through the eyes, soul and spirit of this young Tutsi girl who was brought up in a normal, loving family amongst the rolling green hills of this small nation, Rwanda. It was out of a calm world of normality that evil suddenly gripped the land with such power, hatred and ferociousness. It uncovered man's capacity to become utterly blind and ruthless in the pursuit of ascendant power.

For at least a century there have been ethnic tensions between the Tutsi and Hutu tribes. Since Belgian colonization in the early twentieth century the Tutsis were considered superior to the Hutus, enjoying more opportunities in education and employment than the Hutus causing bitter resentment.

The build-up to the genocide was tangible for the Tutsis; however, nothing could have prepared them for what was about to happen. Frida's Hutu teachers gradually emphasized their prejudices towards the young children in their class, making regular headcounts of those who were Tutsi or Hutu. The Hutu children taunted their Tutsi classmates, as lists of Tutsi names were ominously made for someone, somewhere. The radio station Radio Télévision Libre des Mille Collines (RTLM), owned by top government leaders, began to broadcast veiled messages of hate towards the Tutsis. In the build-up to the genocide the messages became increasingly transparent and threatening. The Tutsis were described as cockroaches and snakes, a chilling parallel to what happened in Nazi Germany when the Jews were dehumanized, justifying extermination. Eventually the radio simply broadcast the frightening message, "Find those Tutsis wherever they are and kill them!"

The catalyst event that is believed to have prompted the start of the genocide happened on the 6th of April, 1994. Juvénal Habyarimana, the President of Rwanda, and Cyprien Ntaryamira, the Hutu President of Burundi, were in an airplane preparing to land at Kigali airport when it was shot down. Both presidents died in the carnage. To this day no one knows who caused the crash, but the Hutus used the event as a powerful propaganda tool to motivate the extremist Hutu groups into action. Within hours the Hutus began their ethnic cleansing, starting the killing of the Tutsis.

It took time for the Hutus to gather momentum and widen the network of the extremist militias. Moderate Hutus opposed to the slaughter were threatened by extremists. Their warning was either to be part of the massacre or be massacred. Neighbor was turned against neighbor. Those who refused to kill were usually killed.

Like all Tutsis, Frida experienced unadulterated fear and terror as she hid and ran from place to place, desperate to escape the machetes and the brutal gang rapes. Friends became enemies and nowhere was safe; no one could be trusted. It all seemed hopeless as the wave of violence came ever closer to home. Eventually the bloodlust of the Hutu militias arrived on Frida's family's doorstep.

What happened next is more than any human being ought to endure. It challenges us to the core and prompts disturbing questions about the nature of man. The question of where God is in the midst of such human depravity becomes more important to Frida. Her journey to answering this is extraordinary. When the militias finally caught up with Frida's family, her mother, father, grandparents, brothers, sister and cousins were all killed. Frida, against all the odds, survived. She more than survived. This story is one of incredible human endurance – mentally, spiritually and physically. Frida discovers a bright light, one so intense that it can pierce and overcome the darkness which sought to destroy so many lives. It is with this hope and message to the world that Frida has written this book. She invites you to share in the dramatic story that transformed a normal home life into a hellish nightmare and yet finishes with her healing and restoration.

ACKNOWLEDGMENTS

I would especially like to thank Sandy Waldron, my editor, for the painstaking work she has carried out in reporting the events and story surrounding my life. The genocide was a gruesome happening in the history of our nation, and it wasn't easy to unravel the complicated journey I experienced. But she has helped me to bring out a true account of my survival and return to normal life, and I owe her a great debt of gratitude. Her patient spirit has been a real example to me.

My thanks are also due to Peter Horrobin of Ellel Ministries and Sovereign World for his initiative and encouragement in wanting to publish my story in order to minister to the Body of Christ the healing and forgiveness which is the unique gift of Jesus to impart. Thank you, too, Peter, for the special personal ministry you had into my life during the memorable time I spent at Ellel Grange.

I would especially like to thank James and Tina Stacey, who in recent years have opened up their home to me and treated me like a daughter with unconditional love and unstinting generosity. In addition, James has carried with me the burden to see my story published and without his help I do not think it would have been possible. Tina has been not only a friend but like a mother to me and a model for life in so many ways.

I would also like to thank Tom White, a young photographer living in Uganda for a year, who took the cover photograph and some of the other photographs in this book. He is a very talented young man and has a great future ahead of him.

My thanks also go to John Whitaker in Public Relations at Ellel Ministries International for his expertise in recording many hours of research in connection with the book.

Chapter 1

THE HOME I LOVED

One of my treasured possessions is a little battered photograph I have of myself as a seven-year-old girl. Everything that belonged to my family was destroyed in the genocide that took place over one hundred days in my country of Rwanda in 1994. It is a picture that belonged to one of my uncles and he gave it to me. It shows me standing in front of our banana plantation at home. I am wearing a simple white dress with blue flowers made for me by my mother. My hair is cropped short, as school rules demanded. I look quite serious, although I remember I was trying to force a smile, but I was worried about what was about to happen. I like the photo because it brings back so many memories.

First, the occasion. The photo is being taken by my uncle who is urging me to smile, but I am more concerned about my mother who is standing just behind the camera. She is furious with me because the previous night – not for the first time or the last – I had stayed at my grandparents' house without telling her and I know that I will shortly have to face her. My mother, Primitive Bamurange, was a strict disciplinarian but she was also very loving. My father, Bernard

Munyabitare, worked away from home, coming back mainly late at night or at weekends, so it was she who primarily created the homely family environment which made my early childhood so happy. The punishment came as I knew it would, but then my misdemeanor was all forgotten and life resumed its normal pattern.

Second, the person I was. I was a serious child, probably overburdened with duties, but full of spark and with a zest for life. I was a bright and conscientious pupil at school – one of the best in my class, even though I was a year younger than the others – and the fastest runner. I grabbed all that life had to offer and, with parents who were keen for their children to have the best possible start in life, I had a great future ahead of me.

Third, and best of all, the family I loved. At this stage (in 1987), my family consisted of Mama and Papa, César (nine years old), me (seven years old), Alestide (four years old) and Régis (two years old), who was my favorite brother. Before he was born, I had longed for a baby to care for and had pestered my mother to provide me with one. As a result when Régis was born, I lavished him with all my care and affection. I also had a sister Solange, who was César's twin, but she lived with my grandparents on the opposite side of the valley.

It seems that when I was born in 1980, Kiki and Mimi, as they were nicknamed, were very put out. They were afraid that this new baby would take their place in our parents' affections and wanted them to take me back to the hospital from which I had come. Their crying was so persistent and their jealousy so intense that in the end my grandmother decided to take them to live with her, which was also a great help to my mother who was looking after three children under two. When Alestide was born, Kiki decided to return home as he now had a brother to play with, but Mimi remained with my grandparents. We saw her often as our homes were not too far apart, but it did mean that I was the only girl at home.

My mother and father were both hardworking and capable people, who provided us with a good standard of living. My father was a businessman and worked most of the time in Kigali, the capital of Rwanda, about fifty miles away, running a wholesale business supplying second-hand clothes to market traders. As a sideline he used his small car as a taxi. As well as our traditional mud-brick home, which he gradually extended over the years, he also built three other houses – one in the Congo, one in our small town of Nyanza and one in Kigali, which he rented out.

My father could be described as something of an entre-preneur. But his business acumen went hand in hand with a very generous heart. I remember many occasions when, on Sundays, knowing my father was home for the weekend, our neighbors would come and ask him for money that they needed to enable their children to receive hospital treatment or to go to school, or for any other problem they might have. Such generosity he had learnt from his own father.

My mother too was a very busy person. As well as looking after the home and plantation with cows, goats, sheep, chicken, ducks and turkeys, helped by a house boy and girl, she tried her hand at various money-making enterprises. One of these was a small shop which she had set up in a room of our house with a door opening out onto the adjacent track. Here she sold the surplus vegetables from our plantation, such as cassava, cabbages, aubergines and avocados, as well as other basic household goods including salt, sugar, rice, soap and paraffin. She also used to run a hairdressing business, which brought a steady stream of women to the house.

My mother's love of people and great trust in them meant

that she often gave her services free of charge and for that reason she never made much money. But we had all we needed at home for my father worked hard to ensure his family was financially secure. "I'm working for you now," he used to say. "When you get older, you will work for yourselves." My father was not a very demonstrative man, but we children all knew that he loved us.

My parents were pillars of our local community. Through their hard work and enterprise they were perhaps better off than our neighbors, but their wealth was never a barrier because they were always so open-hearted. Our neighbors worked in our plantation. When our neighbor's son had a baby, my father lent him one of his cows so that the baby would always have milk. When the cow had a calf, my father gave it to him to keep.

As well as my own home I also loved to be in the home of my godly grandparents, Stephan Munyabitare and Margaret Mukamajoro. When you stayed at their house, you could always guarantee you would go to bed late – and for no other reason than my grandfather's long prayers! It was an unwritten law that if you went to Stephan Munyabitare's house in the evening, before bedtime you prayed! The whole family joined in, as well as their workers and any visitors to the home. It could be very tiring for a little seven-year-old girl, but that never stopped me wanting to be there. I loved my grandfather. He was a man of great integrity who had a tremendous love and care for all kinds of people.

Every time I went to Grandpa's house, there were always people waiting on the steps of his house for him to come out so that they could ask him for money. As a teacher, he was better off perhaps than many, but he gave because he had a heart to give. He was a good man, very kind and very loving. People would often ask him for his advice, particularly married couples who were having problems. Grandpa loved books, but above all he loved the Bible, which he was always reading. Sometimes in the evening people would gather together in front of his house so that he could teach them about the Word of God. He also served in his local Roman Catholic church and led a weekly home group, at which people would read the Bible and pray.

Grandpa was always talking to us as his grandchildren about God. If we didn't go to church on any Sunday, he would want to know why. He taught us never to lie and never to steal, and he explained all the Ten Commandments to us in a way we could really understand. He taught us both by word and by practice, as I discovered to my cost. I remember one day I took my friend's tennis ball without her knowing, because I wanted to play with it. Realizing I would get into severe trouble from my mother if I went home, I went to my grandparents' house – on this occasion, too, without asking her permission. I was having a lovely time playing with the ball when my grandfather came back from work and surprised me. I tried to hide the ball but he asked me, "What are you hiding?"

"Nothing," I lied.

"I know you're hiding something," he said, grabbing hold of me and discovering the ball in my pocket where I had tried to hide it. He wanted to know where I had got the ball, and I told him that my friend had lent it to me so that I could play with it.

"Does your mother know that you are here and that you have this ball?" he then demanded to know.

"Yes," I lied again.

Even though it was already late and not even putting his bags inside the house, he took me straight home. When he discovered that I had stolen the ball, he caned me himself and made me take it back to my friend that very night. I knew I had done wrong and I accepted my punishment.

By the age of seven I had already been attending school for a year. Children did not normally start school until they were seven, but watching my elder brother go to school every day I was desperate to go too. When I was six, my father asked my grandfather to use his influence as a teacher to persuade the headmaster of the local school to allow me to do so. I was very happy and excited to start school, even though it was a wrench to leave my two younger brothers playing happily at home. It was an hour's walk to the Ecole Primaire de Nyakabuye but my brother and I didn't mind, as there were lots of children from our village at the same school and we all walked together.

The noisy chain of chattering children in blue school dresses and blue shirts and khaki shorts hurried its way along the country tracks up and down the hills and through the woods, sometimes in the blistering heat and at other times in the torrential downpours of the rainy season. We knew we were the lucky ones – there were many children whose parents could not afford to send them to school. Our mother gave us strict instructions never to stop on the way to play and never to eat anything given to us by a stranger, because we had to go through an area which was renowned for witchcraft and around that time several children had been poisoned.

In many ways starting school ended the carefree period of my childhood, since from the age of about six and a half my mother said that I was now sufficiently grown up to do a lot of work around the house. In term-time I would leave home early because each morning, of my own volition, I went to the six o'clock Mass at the Roman Catholic Church, where I was a server. Although the church was fairly near my school, I would still have to run hard to make sure I arrived by 7.30 a.m. when class started, as late children would be severely punished. This I did barefoot, since we weren't allowed to wear shoes so that poor children were not at a disadvantage.

When school finished at midday, we did the hour-walk back home, and then my brothers and I had to water the vegetables and flowers in my mother's gently sloping garden, which meant that we had to fetch water from the standpipe three miles away. If we could, we would save ourselves the walk by finding a small stream and draw the water from there. It was always a great relief when it was the rainy season! Then, while my brothers played, I had to face a pile of dishes which awaited my return in the kitchen. And after that I had to settle down to my homework.

Harder to bear were my duties in the school holidays when, while my brothers played football or visited our cousins or their friends, I, as the only girl living at home, was required to do the housework and our workers, who normally did these jobs, were given a holiday.

"It's not fair," I would complain to my mother. "Why can't I go and play like César and Alestide?"

"You are the only girl here," she would say. "I want to be certain that if anything happened to me, you would be able to take care of your brothers. And I certainly don't want you to grow up to be one of those silly girls who are good for nothing."

The thought that she might die really worried me and once I asked her, "Are you sick, Mama?"

"No," she replied, "but it happens to other people and it could easily happen to me."

I was shocked by her reply, and from that time I always prayed that God would never let me see the death of any of my family members but let me die before them.

So, while my brothers had fun, I would trudge the three arduous miles to the standpipe with a bucket of clothes on my head and a gerry can in my hand. On the way back, as well as the clean clothes I would carry a gerry-can full of the water I needed to clean the house and cook dinner. The standpipe was in quite a remote place in the valley and I didn't like being alone there. People would talk about the snakes they had seen and I always felt on tenterhooks in case one should appear. Fortunately I only ever encountered dead ones. Some days my task was made a little lighter by the companionship of a neighbor's eight-year-old daughter who would come to do her family's washing. At least then we could chat as we worked and the place where we did the washing did not seem quite so scary and the long walk back did not seem quite so lonely. If I did not complete all the jobs my mother had given me, she would give me a severe beating.

I hated staying at home while my brothers had all the fun. I hated being the only girl at home and wished that my sister Mimi could come back home and help me. She was so lucky to live with my grandparents and my father's twin sisters, Martha and Mary, who were in their twenties. I was so often jealous of the life of luxury that she lived and secretly thought that she was spoilt. So many times I wished I could be a boy because it was obvious to me at that time that boys were better than girls.

When it all got too much for me I would cry my heart out and plead and plead with my mother to let me have time to play. Sometimes she would put her hand on my arm and say, "It's not because I don't love you that I am treating you in this way. It's because I want to teach you how to do things properly." Occasionally she would give me one or two days to go and stay with my friends or my cousins. Often, so reluctant was I to return to my work at home that I eked the visit out a bit longer than she had said and then, when I did return home, she would really punish me once again.

Whenever I did have a chance to play, I preferred to play with boys rather than girls. I would play football with my brothers and ride on the bike we all shared. Of course, we would sometimes fight, as all children do, but there was a strong and loving bond between my brothers and I, especially with Régis. Régis was a very loving boy. He was mad on cows and wanted to be a herdsman when he grew up. We were always being co-opted into the role of cow so he could herd us around, and he would cry if we refused to play along. As the family joker Alestide was always making us laugh and was very popular among the boys at school. Physically, however, he was not very strong and he was often ill with malaria and other sicknesses.

With my father frequently away, my eldest brother César was very happy to step into his shoes, a role my mother encouraged. He loved being the "big man" and going off to market to do the shopping and he was always our protector at school. Each day he made sure that we all got home safely from school, particularly in the rainy season when the rivers were swollen and very dangerous. I, for my part, would enjoy mothering my brothers, checking, for example, that they took their jumpers to school in case it should rain and hurrying them along so that we weren't late.

At the time I resented being the only girl and having to do so much of the work around the home, but looking back I can see that my mother's early training provided me with the skills I needed to survive in the days that lay ahead.

I wish I could transport you back into that photo I have described for you and give you some idea of the beauty and tranquility of my remote home sheltering in the hillside. They call Rwanda the country of a thousand hills and as I looked out from my home, the gentle rolling hills stretched away in every direction. They were lush and green and provided the perfect setting for our rural farming community.

Dotted across the hills, spread wide apart, were the small mud-brick homes of our neighbors, each with their pan-tiled roofs. Depending on the size of their land, each would have a small plantation growing the cassava, maize, bananas, beans and tomatoes they needed for food. For many this was their only source of income and they were grateful for opportunities to work for people like my father and my grandfather with more land and earn a little cash to supplement their income, and that is why it was so hard for many of them to cover the extras that life threw at them at every turn. From our house you could see Felecita's tiny house in the valley to the right and, over to the left, much further up the slope, in a clump of three simple dwellings, was the home of Vitale, who was to play a huge part in my story.

High up at the top of the opposite side of the valley to my house was my grandfather's house. To get to it, we walked down past the huge avocado tree (by which I am standing in the photo), past my mother's extensive banana plantation, past the cassava plants and the sweet potatoes, then past the area where my mother grew her tomatoes, aubergines and cabbages – and my father had dug out a sizeable water tank to grow fish for food – over the small stream in the valley and began the slow, tortuous climb up the other side. We hated that climb and as children we would stand in a long line, pushing each other up, but it was worth it when you got there because there was always a warm welcome waiting for you and invariably a plate of home-cooked food. Grandma's food always seemed to taste so much better than the food at home – much to my mother's annoyance.

There was no fear in the Rwanda of those days of my childhood. The community was at one. Our neighbors were our friends. The hills rang with the sound of my brothers' voices – in the hills sound carries for miles – as they played football on the meadow in the valley a short walk away, or swam in my father's fish tank. Making a living was not easy, but the community worked together for the good of everyone. That was the home I loved, but which is now lost to me forever.

Chapter 2

SHADOWS

"Good morning, Mr Headmaster," the class chanted, rising to their feet as Mr Morris came into the room. He was very strict at the best of times and classes would fall silent at the mere sight of him. Today his expression was even more severe than usual and I noticed his bald head was glistening with sweat. He immediately instructed the class, "Hutus, stand up."

About two-thirds of the children stood up confidently, looking around at their classmates who remained seated. As young as they were, they sensed the strength of their position. Mr Morris counted the children standing and, motioning for them to sit down, then ordered, "Tutsis, stand."

I had made up my mind that I would stand when my three best friends, Claudette, Sophie and Honorette, stood up, but when Honorette had stood up as a Hutu, Claudette had motioned to me not to stand, leaving me feeling confused. I was not really sure which tribe I belonged to, but I knew I must be the same as Claudette, because she was my best friend. I hesitated. Seeing Claudette stand as a Tutsi, I decided to stand too. Just at that moment the headmaster barked, "Come on. Be quick about it. I don't need any of your silly behavior." This caused the Hutu children who had stood moments before to laugh at us and left me feeling very cheap. My legs were trembling. Finally the headmaster told the children who belonged to Rwanda's third tribe, the Batwa, a tiny minority of the population, to stand and a couple of children did so.

The headmaster made a round of all the classes in the school asking the same questions and after school, as we made our way home, the talk was all about who had stood with whom. We now knew something our parents had never told us: we knew who was a Hutu and who was a Tutsi. The reason, I discovered, why Claudette knew she was a Tutsi whereas I didn't, was because her father often spoke about the fact that he had almost been killed as a boy during a period of great trouble for the Tutsis after the Tutsi king, Rudahigwa, had died in 1959. Not only were Claudette and I best friends, but our mothers were best friends too. I hated what had happened that morning and wished that the headmaster had not come to our classroom. It changed things somehow and, although we all still played together very happily, there was a lurking feeling that we were not the same.

The head count of Hutus and Tutsis came to be a three-monthly occurrence, as the headmaster complied with the government's directive, and each time it happened it reinforced my feeling of dread. Each time the Hutu children would laugh at us and goad us, and neither the headmaster nor our teacher would make any attempt to shut them up. I hated the sound they made and the atmosphere it created so much that on one occasion I even attempted my own silent protest and remained sitting quietly in my seat while the Tutsis were being counted. Noticing that I had remained seated, my teacher said, "Stand up, you stupid girl," and I had no other choice but to stand and be counted with the other Tutsi children.

Being a Hutu or a Tutsi had never been an issue in our family. In fact, it was something that was never even talked about. One of my father's best friends and his business partner, Vincent Nzigiyimfura, was a Hutu, as were many of our neighbors. When my parents held a party in the village hall to celebrate a family occasion, such as each of their children receiving First Communion, it was a mixture of Hutu and Tutsi friends who came.

Many Hutu children came to our house to play, and we would play at theirs. My mother was a respected member of the community. Many young women who were getting married would ask her to be their matron, which in our custom was a kind of mentor and supporter in their married life. This she was pleased to do for Tutsi and Hutu alike. She also taught us to care for all our elderly neighbors by taking them meals and fruit when they were not well and helping them with any jobs they needed doing. Tribe had never been an issue, and I could not understand why it mattered. I wanted it all to go away.

But it did not go away. Bit by bit things were changing in Rwanda, and I was scared. My fear intensified a few months later when, one Tuesday evening while we were waiting for the weekly play which we always listened to as a family to come on the radio, we heard a disturbing news report. The date was 2 October 1990. The previous day Tutsi rebels led by Fred Rwigema had attacked Rwanda from their base in Uganda. The report claimed that the rebels were being supported by Tutsis from within the country and it warned that these people – these "cockroaches" or "snakes", as the newsreader called them – would be rooted out and punished. I thought they were talking about real cockroaches and real snakes invading the country and was terrified by the idea. Although they tried to play it down, we could see that our parents were clearly shaken by this news report. They did not want to explain the situation to us, and we were left feeling alarmed and frightened.

Later that evening, out of our parents' hearing, we children talked about what we had heard. My elder brother Kiki, who was now twelve and often talked with the other boys at school about the political situation, took the lead. "Don't you know," he said, "that in 1959 there was a war, as a result of which many Tutsis were forced to leave Rwanda and live in other countries?"

I vaguely recalled something we had learnt in our history lessons.

"They are the ones who are now coming back into the country," he continued, "and there is going to be another war!"

He tried to sound as if he understood what was going on, but I'm sure he didn't. His words, however, fuelled my anxiety, and that night I could not sleep. In the morning, convinced that we were all going to be killed, I refused to go to school. Mama tried to make light of the situation and tried to reassure me that there wasn't going to be any war. She said the rebels they were talking about were not human beings but small animals with long ears, and there was nothing to worry about. But I could see that she was lying and in her face I could see that she was afraid too. My father added his own words of reassurance that nothing was going to happen and life would just go on as it always had. I wished I could believe them.

When we arrived at school, there were groups of children standing together, discussing the news. It's not just me that's worried, I thought to myself. The atmosphere was tense. Was it just a coincidence that it was the day for the headmaster to come into class and carry out his head count once again? Once

again, as the Tutsi children stood, the Hutus shouted and
jeered at us, and the headmaster made no attempt to make
them be quiet. On this occasion, however, our teacher, who
was a Hutu, brought them to order.

Later that day, when I got home, I asked my mother a
stupid question. "Mama," I asked, "why did you choose to be
Tutsi? Didn't you know it was a bad tribe?"

"We did not choose it, my child," she replied. "We were
born Tutsi. Nobody chooses what tribe they want to be. God
makes you the way He wants you, and you can't complain
about it." Her voice was trembling, and I could see that she
was on the verge of tears.

✤   ✤   ✤

In the days that followed I came to understand that the Tutsis
who had been forced to flee in the early 1960s during a
prolonged period of violence against them, in which many
thousands were massacred and thousands more were forced
from their homes, had been asking the government for
permission to return home. These exiled Tutsis numbered in
their hundreds of thousands – probably in excess of 700,000
people. The government had refused, saying that the country
was too small to accommodate such an influx.

The frustration of those forced to live in exile had grown
over time until they declared that if they were not permitted
to return in peace they would come in war. Tutsis living as
refugees in the Congo, Burundi and Uganda banded together
to form the Rwanda Patriotic Front (RPF), based in Uganda.
As we had heard on that first alarming news report, the
government was accusing Tutsis within the country, particularly businessmen and other wealthy Tutsis, of giving them
support, thus enabling them to buy guns and other arms.

Towards the end of that same academic year we arrived

home from school one day to find no one at home. Although quite unusual, we were not particularly worried. The house was locked but we knew where Mama left the key and we let ourselves in. We were a bit surprised that she had not left a message as she normally did. A little while later one of our neighbors, Felecita, who used to work for Mama when she needed her in the plantation, came running over to ask if Mama or Papa were back yet. We replied that Mama wasn't back yet, but that Papa was in Kigali. She gave us some shocking news.

"Your father came back earlier today after you'd left for school and then, not long afterwards, soldiers came to arrest him. They've taken him away."

"Where did the soldiers take him?" Kiki asked.

"I don't know," she replied. "That's where your mother has gone – to try and find out where your father's been taken and see if she can find someone to help her get him out."

"But what did Papa do?" I asked.

"I really don't know, Frida," she replied, adding, "Let's just wait and see what your mother is able to tell us when she comes back."

Mama didn't get back until late that evening. At about 9 o'clock there was a knock at the door and we all ran to open it. "Who is it?" we asked through the door, because she had always taught us never to open the door unless we knew the person who was there.

"It's me, my children," she said.

As soon as we heard her voice, we opened the door and we fell over each other as we all tried to greet her at the same time. She looked very tired. With her were our two cousins Sebakara and Adam Laurgin, whom she had asked to walk with her through the field which was a short cut to our house. After thanking the brothers and telling them to go straight back home as it was late, Mama sat down and we brought her something to eat, thinking that she must be very hungry. Then, unable to wait a moment longer, we asked, "What's happened, Mama? Where's Papa?"

"Papa has been put in prison," she told us, "but don't worry, because he'll be back very soon."

"Why, Mama?" I asked. "It's because he's a Tutsi, isn't it?"

"No," she said. "They're accusing him of giving aid to the rebels, but I've asked Vincent Nzigiyimfura to help him and we'll prove that it's not true. He's OK, and I'm sure he'll be released very soon."

It was horrible to think of my father being in prison, accused of something I felt sure he had not done. For our mother's sake we stemmed the tide of questions which we were all longing to ask and for once we took ourselves off to bed.

It was in fact three more days before my father was released. My mother had begged his Hutu business partner Vincent to help him and I think a bribe was probably paid. It was, however, not the end of the matter and my father was subjected to ongoing intimidation and threats, and he knew he was being watched. He decided to work mainly in Nyanza and to go to Kigali only when it was really necessary. He also sold his car in an attempt to play down his wealth and success as a businessman. In any case, traveling around Rwanda was becoming more and more difficult, and in order to leave the district everyone had to apply for permission. It goes without saying that permission was granted far more readily to Hutus than it was to Tutsis.

The more we heard about what was going on, the more we realized that my father had got off lightly. Some people who were arrested never made it out of prison again, having been beaten to death. Others were subjected to a long, slow death by having paraffin poured into their ear, which gradually burned its way through their body. Of those who did emerge from prison, a great many were never the same again.

Not long after my father had been released I awoke late one evening disturbed by unusual noises. Since my father had extended the house, I had my own bedroom in the main house with my parents, and my brothers shared another small house next door. As I entered the living room, I was shocked to see my father stagger into the house and then collapse onto the floor. He had been badly beaten and was covered in blood. He had been riding his bicycle along the isolated country roads home from work when he had been attacked, beaten with sticks to within an inch of his life and then the top of his little finger on his right hand had been brutally cut off.

I was terrified, expecting his attackers to storm into the house at any moment. Mama desperately tried to persuade him to let her take him to hospital but Papa would not hear of it. Although hardly able to speak, he made her understand that his attackers, none of whom he had recognized, had warned him of even worse consequences if he told anyone about the attack and if they ever saw him on the road again at night. Mama bathed his wounds and bandaged them as best she could and in the morning she took him to the hospital. They said that he had had an accident on his bike on his way home from work. '

Around the same time Papa's cousin Rurangna Gracien suffered a similar attack and three of his fingers were cut off. They were the lucky ones – many people died in such attacks. These incidents were never reported. Whom could they report them to? After that Papa started coming home earlier. My mother warned us not to say a word at school about what had been happening.

A month or so later family life was rocked once again by the news that my mother's two brothers had also been arrested. One day, while my mother was visiting her friend, Donatilla, a young man whom I didn't know very well, arrived with a message for her. Since he seemed very tense and troubled, I decided to run and fetch my mother straightaway. We arrived back home to find him waiting impatiently outside the house. In private he told her that Uncle Narcisse and Uncle Emile had been arrested that morning, also accused of helping the rebels. The young man was in a hurry to get back as he also faced the risk of being arrested and needed to get to safety.

Mama tried to hide the news from us but we could see that she was very upset and desperately worried about the two brothers she loved so much. That evening she went over to tell my grandparents about it, but there was nothing anyone could do except hope and pray. Much later we heard that after weeks and weeks in prison where they were tortured, the two men were released. They immediately decided to flee the country and go to Burundi. The younger brother stayed there, but the elder brother went to join the RPF on the borders of Uganda. My mother never saw them again.

These were years of great tension for the people of Rwanda. Sometimes things would seem almost normal, and then we would hear of another person being imprisoned, another person being beaten up, another person disappearing. Even more devastating was news of large numbers of Tutsis being massacred. The first massacre had occurred in October 1990, and there were two more in 1991 and another two in 1992. Although we knew it was Hutus who were carrying out these attacks against our tribe, somehow we could not equate them with the people among whom we had lived so harmoniously for so long, alongside whom we sat in church, with whom we played in the playground.

Although as a young girl there was no way I could appreciate the grave implications of the evil that was tightening its grip on our country, I lived every day with the fear that cast its shadow over our lives. I saw it in my parents' faces, I heard it in whispered conversations, I sensed it in the adjustments we were having to make to our lives.

Our days at Nyakabuye School which had begun so happily ended abruptly and cruelly. The whole family had attended a requiem mass for my father's uncle's wife held early in the morning and my brother, my sister and I had run for all we were worth to try and make it to school on time, arriving just five minutes late. Breathless we explained our reason for being late, but no notice was taken by the woman teacher who was on late duty that morning. She was a Hutu. Together with some other children who had also been late, we were forced to walk on our knees along a long stony path all the way to our seat in our classrooms. Each time we fell over with the pain, the teacher beat us with a stick. After a while she dismissed some of the other children and allowed them to return to their classes. These children were Hutus.

As the stones pressed into our knees, the pain was excruciating, not to mention the humiliation and sense of unfairness we felt. At one point Kiki suggested that we should get up and go home, but Mimi said that our parents would just think we were being disobedient to the teachers and would punish us even more. "No, they wouldn't," Kiki said. "They know we were at the mass." Hearing them talking, the teacher intervened angrily. Once again Kiki tried to explain that there was a good reason why we were late for school that morning, but she just slapped him across the face and told him he was lying. "Well, you can choose," she continued. "If you don't want to walk on your knees, I will cane you instead." We could see the hatred in her eyes as she caned each of us in turn.

When we arrived home that lunchtime, we were all dejected and very, very sore. I burst into tears as we explained what had happened to Mama. Both our parents were very angry at the punishment we had received which was clearly excessive. Mama insisted that Papa needed to change our schools before the next school year. He agreed with her, but the words he spoke next made a deep and lasting impression on me. "We can change their school," he said, "but the problem is not going to go away." At that moment I understood that the harsh punishment we had received had not been about being late, but had been because we were Tutsis. I didn't say anything, but recognition dawned in my heart.

The next day Papa went into the school to talk to the headmaster. He was very angry and ready for a fight – even a physical one. Since the headmaster wasn't around, he had to make do with voicing his complaint to one of the teachers. When he was told that the punishment we had received was in line with the policy of the school, he declared there and then, "Right. I am taking my children out of this school. They will not be coming back here ever again." That was fine, as far as we were concerned.

Chapter 3

BORN AT THE WRONG TIME

The following school year Kiki, Mimi, Alestide and I started at Gatagara Primary School, which was the school my grandfather had taught at prior to his retirement earlier that year. Régis was already attending the nursery at the school as my Aunt Clemence was one of the teachers. Gatagara Primary School was a school for disabled children, but it did have a few able-bodied pupils. My grandfather used his influence with the headmaster, who was married to his niece, to get us a place at the school. We were very happy to be going there. Not only was it a very good school with a Tutsi headmaster, but it was much nearer home – only a twenty-minute walk away. Another bonus was that it did not have a school uniform, and I enjoyed being able to wear what I liked. And, of course, when the head count came round again, no shouting or name-calling was tolerated from the Hutu children!

I was sad to have left behind my good friends Claudette and Sophie – our other friend Honorette had died of malaria the previous year. It had been very hard to lose a friend we loved so much. In my new class I was lucky to have four cousins, Valérie, Yvette, Eric and Olivier. Eric and Olivier had changed

schools at the same time as us to go to one nearer to their
home. Our teacher Cécile was a Tutsi and there was an equal
number of Hutus and Tutsis in the class. Cécile was an
excellent teacher, treating everyone the same and only
punishing children when it was really necessary.

It was an important year for Kiki and Mimi because it was
their final year at primary school, in which they would have to
prepare for their national examination. That year the school
system nationally was due to change and the amount of years
children spent in primary school was being reduced from
eight to six. That meant that I, now aged twelve, should be
taking the national examination at the same time as the twins.
However, since I was already a year younger than my
classmates, my parents felt that I was not ready to leave home
to go to boarding school (which was the normal pattern for
brighter students), and so at the new school they made me
repeat Year 5. I wasn't at all happy to be put back a year with
children who, although my age, seemed much younger than
me, especially when I felt ready to take the exam, but I knew I
had to respect my parents' decision. Being in a new school
with good teachers made up for my initial disappointment.

Since our previous academic year had been so disrupted,
Papa arranged for us all to have some private tuition after
school on Tuesdays and Thursdays, together with the cousins
who were in my class. For this we went down to a school for
blind children where our tutor taught. It didn't really help as
Kiki and Mimi both failed the exam. Failing the exam was not
particularly unusual, since there weren't enough public
schools to accommodate all the bright pupils and the places
did not always go to the most deserving! Many gifted Tutsi
children were passed over in favor of less able Hutus. Both
Kiki and Mimi went on to private secondary schools in
Nyanza, Mimi choosing to study Commerce and Accounts

at one school and Kiki Car Mechanics at another. Papa bought them bicycles to enable them to get to school, as it was much too far to walk. Since Mimi still lived with my grandparents, the twins would meet up along the road and ride together. Sometimes, if Papa wasn't particularly busy, they would meet him for lunch in Nyanza. Now that he was no longer able to go to Kigali, Papa's business was gradually going downhill. He tried to put a brave face on it, but at times I could tell that he was deeply troubled.

Each afternoon I would try and make sure that my two little brothers Alestide and Régis did their homework. I had no problems with Régis who was doing well at school, but Alestide found school work quite hard and was always trying to come up with a way to avoid doing it. Sometimes he would hide his homework or he would fall asleep when he was meant to be doing it. If I got angry with him, he would always cry and apologize, and then I would feel sorry and do it for him. His teachers could not understand why, when his homework was always so good, he would often fail his exams.

About this time I began to realize that Mama was pregnant again. Nobody had said anything about it, but I could see that her body was changing and I put two and two together. I was very happy about the prospect of a new baby in the family. Without saying anything, I looked out the clothes that Régis had worn as a baby and washed them and hung them on the line.

"What are you going to do with those little clothes?" Mama asked, obviously surprised.

"We're going to have a baby, aren't we?" I replied.

"Who told you we're going to have a baby?" she wanted to know.

"Nobody," I said. "I just saw for myself."

"What a grown-up girl you have become!" she exclaimed.

"You're right. We are going to have a baby. What would you like it to be – a boy or a girl?"

"A girl, of course!" I said without a moment's hesitation. "There are enough boys in this house." Then I added, "When she grows up, perhaps she can help me with the housework."

Mama smiled and said, "Well, let's wait and see. Whether it's a boy or a girl, God gives us what He wants, not what we want."

A few months later Papa fell ill with a problem affecting the blood vessels in his feet which caused them to swell. He was in terrible pain and had to remain in bed the whole time. By now Mama was heavily pregnant. It worried me to see her working so hard. She was obviously becoming more and more tired, and the strain of managing the house and plantation as well as taking care of Papa was taking its toll on her. Although it was near exam time I suggested that I could take a few days off school to help her, which would release the houseboy to undertake some of the heavier work in the plantation. To my surprise she agreed, and I was very glad to be able to make life a bit easier for her. This time I didn't complain about doing the cooking, cleaning, washing, etc. because I knew I was helping Mama, Papa and the baby.

A week later, not long after the whole family had gone to bed at our normal time of 7 o'clock, something woke me. I immediately became aware that Mama was struggling with her breathing and I went to see if she was all right. She looked terrible, and she was experiencing great difficulty trying to get out of bed. Papa was so ill that he could not help her in any way.

Gasping for breath she told me to go and fetch her things from the cupboard. All women in our village would prepare themselves in case they went into labor in the middle of the night and could not get to hospital in time. I knew where Mama had put the things she would need for the labor and ran to get them. The thought of leaving her even for a minute terrified me. Looking back I think it was probably just normal labor pains, but at the time I was convinced she was going to die.

When I got back I found her trying to make her way to our outside washroom, which was a very small room with a concrete floor and no roof. Since she could hardly move I needed to help her. As soon as we reached the washroom she told me to run and wake Kiki and our houseboy Cyprien and tell them to fetch our grandmother, and then to heat up some water. This I did, but rather than Grandma I told the boys to fetch our neighbor Felecita. I was afraid that by the time they got to Grandma's house Mama might have died.

Then I lit the fire in the kitchen, which was no easy task, and put the water on to boil, all the while praying that God would save Mama and the baby. As soon as this was done, I ran back to Mama. At that very moment she let out an excruciating scream and I could see she was in terrible pain. I started to cry. I didn't know what to do. Five minutes later she screamed again and this time I heard a baby's cry. It was 12.25 a.m. I made as if to move nearer to her, but she told me to leave her until she had finished what she was doing. I didn't really understand what she meant but I did as she asked. As I left the washroom there was a loud knock at the door and I went to answer it. It was the boys returning with Felecita, who went straight into Mama. I heard another agonizing scream and I really thought she was going to die. Felecita shouted, "It's OK now. It's all over," and the baby cried again. I felt an immense joy wash over me.

Felecita called for me to bring the hot water. As I took it in,

I caught a glimpse of the baby and I longed to hold it, but I could see it was not the right moment. "Is it a boy or a girl?" I whispered. In a very tired voice Mama replied, "It's a girl, just as you wanted, Frida." Returning to the other room where my brothers were waiting, I jumped for joy and told them that we had a sister. They smiled and relaxed, glad that it was all over.

As I went back into the main house, Papa called out to me, asking if the baby was born and whether it was a boy or a girl. "It's a girl, a beautiful girl," I told him, even though I hadn't actually seen her yet.

I hovered outside the washroom in case they needed anything. After a little while, Felecita brought the baby out and handed her to me. She was now dressed and swaddled in a soft blanket. Calling to Kiki to bring the lamp, I took her quickly into the house so that she would not get cold. Once inside, the boys all gathered round to see her for the first time. As we uncovered her face which was buried in the blanket, we saw that she was absolutely beautiful.

Hearing our voices, Papa shouted to me to bring the baby to him. As he held her in his arms, he said to her, "You are a real surprise!" I think he was referring both to the fact that they had not expected to have another baby after Régis and that she had come so unexpectedly during the night, giving no sign the previous day that she was about to be born. His voice was very flat, and I could not understand why he was not rejoicing in the birth of his baby as we were.

For the rest of the night Mama and baby slept in my bed and I slept on a mattress by their side, so that I could help Mama with anything she needed. Before I fell asleep, I asked her, "Mama, do you think I could stay with you again today and not go to school for one more day?"

"No, Frida," she replied. "You've done enough, and you've

got your national exam coming up. You should go to school. Grandma will come over and help me. But thank you for being so courageous tonight."

On the way to school that day I could not help but tell everyone I met that my Mama had had a baby, even if they didn't ask me. It was 18 March 1993. Four days earlier I had celebrated my thirteenth birthday and in five days' time Alestide would be ten. I liked the fact that we were all going to be having our birthday in the same month.

For several weeks after she was born my baby sister had no name. We just used to call her "Bébé." As time went on, Mama complained to Papa, "Why aren't you giving the baby a name?" Papa looked very sad and said, "I have no name for this baby." Then in our language of Kinyarwanda he spoke the word *gatesi*, meaning "careless" or "reckless." By that he meant that she had been born at the wrong time.

"What kind of name is that for my child?" Mama said. "Can't you think of another name? Give her a good name."

"No, there is no other name that I can give her. She is Gatesi."

That same day, wanting my little sister to have a prettier name, I looked up the feast-day for the day she was born, which was the Feast of St Bénédicte. So she became Gatesi Bénédicte, but everyone called her by the name my father had given her: "Gatesi."

In June that year I took my national examination and to my great excitement I passed it. I was given a place at a boarding school in Byimana which was a two-hour bus drive from home, with quite a long walk from our house to the bus stop. Since it was my father's old school, I had heard a lot about it, and it had been my dream to go there. The following

September I left home with a mixture of sadness and anticipation.

My father took me to the school and helped me settle in. To his surprise he discovered that the school still had the same headmaster as when he was a boy – a stately old Belgian. I quickly made friends with a girl called Oda who was also new to the school. We were in the same dormitory, sharing it with ten other girls, and soon became very close. I also met another of my cousins, Karaba, although we didn't realize we were related until her parents came to visit her and made the connection.

In December we had our first holiday and I looked forward to seeing how my little baby sister had grown. When I had left home she was a strong and happy five-month-old baby. When the bus arrived in Nyanza, I was pleased to see Kiki waiting for me with his bike, because I had been wondering how I would manage to carry my bag home. I plied him with questions about how everyone was doing and he replied that everyone was fine. Whatever question I asked, he never seemed to mention Gatesi, and I found it odd. "Is Gatesi walking yet?" I asked. His answer was evasive, and he quickly changed the subject by asking about my journey and about how I was getting on at school. It reminded me of when Mama had come to see me at school in November. She too had seemed to skirt round all the questions I had asked about the baby.

When we arrived home, we found Mama sitting on a chair outside the house. She didn't look at all well. After we had greeted one another, I immediately asked where Gatesi was. "You'll see her. Don't worry," Mama replied. "Have a rest first." This was very unlike my mother who would normally have given me work to do the moment I walked in the house – now she was being nice to me and forcing me to rest!

While Mama was fetching me some food, I impatiently asked

Alestide where the baby was. "Is she over at Grandma's?"
I asked him.

"Mama will tell you later," he told me.

I knew something was wrong.

As soon as I woke up from my nap, I went to find Mama.
She was in her room.

"What's happened to Gatesi?" I asked.

"I can't keep the truth from you any longer," she replied.
"But I need you to be strong, as we have all had to be."

At that moment the horrible thought crossed my mind that
Gatesi might be dead, but I quickly brushed it away. I couldn't
believe that she could have even been sick without anyone
telling me.

"What's happened, Mama?" I asked again.

"I don't know how to tell you this, Frida," Mama said, "but
Gatesi is dead. She died in October, but be strong." The tears
were running down her face and she could hardly finish her
sentence.

I burst into tears and ran out of the room. How could they
possibly not have told me that my little sister had died! How
could they have buried her without me being there? Didn't I
matter in this family? I felt very angry and very hurt. Shut out.

My mother followed me into my room. She was crying too.
"I'm very sorry we didn't tell you, Frida. It was your first term
in your secondary school and we didn't want to make it even
more difficult for you. We knew you would be heart-broken.
Forgive me. I'm very sorry. I know you really loved her, I just
couldn't tell you."

"Why did you keep on lying to me when I got here?" I burst
out.

"I didn't want to tell you the bad news as soon as you got
here. You've been away a long time. There is no way I could
tell you the moment you arrived."

I was devastated. Kiki took me to see Gatesi's grave and for days and days I cried and cried. It was two days before I was able to ask my mother what had caused Gatesi's death. She told me that they had taken her to hospital with malaria. Although she was ill her condition was not critical. Since as a baby the medicine could not be given in tablet form, they decided to put her on a drip. Her arms were still too small for the drip to be inserted, so it had to be put straight into her head. My parents believed that the Hutu doctor administering the injection into her head had deliberately twisted it so that she would die. Her condition deteriorated rapidly immediately after the drip had been inserted. In those days not many Tutsis who went into hospital came out alive.

The days of that holiday passed by in a blur as I struggled to come to terms with the loss of my little sister. I had expected to spend all my free time playing with her in the garden and her absence left a huge hole.

The tragedy of her death and the continuing tension in the country were taking their toll on my parents too. There was a great deal of unrest in Kigali, fuelled by clashes between rival political parties which erupted into riots. There were increasing incidents of people being killed by bombs which had been planted in crowded places and hand grenades being thrown into taxi-buses or passing cars. Although my father no longer worked in Kigali, he did need to make occasional trips into the city to conduct his business. If my father was ever late home from work, Mama would become extremely agitated. Kiki and I would try to keep her company as she waited anxiously for him, but we often found it very hard to keep our eyes open.

The trouble spread to Nyanza, and my mother was constantly warning us to be on the look-out for danger. She told us to be wary of the people we were sitting next to in the taxi buses and to be on the look-out for bags where bombs might be hidden. I was scared to death one day when I almost got caught up in a riot and, whenever I could, I preferred to stay within the refuge of our home.

My father tried to keep in touch with what was happening by listening to the radio. In secret he would listen to Radio Muhabura which was the station of the *Inkotanyi* (the RPF), but knowing how dangerous it would be if he were caught, having already been accused of being a collaborator, as a smokescreen he would also listen to Radio Télévision Libre des Mille Collines (RTLM),[1] which had come on air during 1993. It was a propaganda machine which delivered a message of hate against the Tutsis and, as time went on, it saw less and less need to veil its aim of seeing the whole tribe exterminated.

We began to hear rumors that lists had been compiled of the Tutsis who were to be killed. I even heard that my old headmaster Mr Morris from Nyakabuye School had been involved in drawing them up. When I arrived back at school after the Christmas holidays my Hutu classmates began to taunt me that I was on one of these lists and that it would not be long before I would be dead. "One day we are going to kill you," they kept saying. It was horrible. The Hutu girls in our dormitory also began to turn nasty, and Oda and I asked for permission to move in with some older Tutsi girls we knew in another dormitory, but our request was refused. Going back to the dormitory began to be quite an ordeal and there were many nights when I lay awake, terrified in case one of the girls put their menacing threats into action.

My worst fears were confirmed by an incident that happened at the school. We were all in the dining room one

1. Thousand Hills Independent Radio and Television.

evening when there was a power cut. In the darkness the Hutu children started chanting, "Kill the Tutsis ... Kill the Tutsis ... " I was really scared and hid under one of the tables. When the lights came back on, it was discovered that a Tutsi boy called Eric had been stabbed with a knife during the blackout. The wound wasn't serious, but there was blood everywhere, and all the Tutsi children were very shaken.

Shortly afterwards my father came to see me and I told him what had happened. He comforted me by saying that it must have been an accident and that nothing was going to happen at school. His words went some way to reassuring me and after his visit I felt a bit calmer.

I was very glad when the term ended and it was time to go home for the Easter holidays. I was happy to be with my family again. I did not know that by the time I went back to that school my whole life would have been torn apart.

Chapter 4

"Kill Them All"

It was 7 April 1994 – a Thursday. I was soon to go back to school and my parents were planning to make a trip into Nyanza that morning to buy me all the things I would need. Listening to the radio as we usually did, we heard the news that would put an end to our family life forever. The news reader solemnly announced that the President of Rwanda, Juvenal Habyarima, a Hutu, was dead. His plane had been shot down while preparing to land at Kigali airport the previous evening. The President of Burundi had died with him. The news had already been broadcast the night before but we had not heard it. The announcement concluded with the ominous instruction that everyone should remain where they were until further notice.

We children jumped up and down with joy. "Hurrah!" we shouted. "The President is dead. Now we'll get to go to the good schools! Now we'll have the opportunities we couldn't have before!"

"Be quiet!" my father snapped. "You don't know what you're talking about. This is the worst possible thing that could have happened. This is going to mean serious trouble for us – and I mean serious."

Of course, we were too young to understand what he meant, but later on, when we were on our own, Kiki said to me, "I understand what Papa meant. We are on the list and we are going to die."

"No, no, no, it's not possible," I protested. "It could only happen if they sent soldiers into the area. Our neighbors wouldn't kill us. There is no way that they would kill us. We're not going to die."

One of our parents' friends, Marie Rose, who was Mimi's godmother, was at our house. She had moved out of the district and had come back to pay us a visit. When the announcement came on the radio, she became very agitated. "I'm not staying here," she said, "I must get back to my husband and my children." She was married to a Hutu. Mama tried to stop her, fearing she might be killed on the way home but she grabbed her bag and left.

Shortly afterwards Papa went into Nyanza to find out what was happening. It was not long before he came back, looking very grave. "Things are very bad," he said. "There are roadblocks everywhere. All the arrangements are in place for the killing to begin." My parents had given up trying to pretend that everything was going to be OK. Later that day my father and some other Tutsi men had a meeting at which they agreed that they would defend their families if the Hutus came. They would not attack anyone, but they would not stand by while their families were murdered.

From that night on, fearing that our house might be burnt down while we were sleeping, we slept out in the forest close by. Mama told us to put on several layers of clothes – a couple of pairs of trousers and two or three jumpers on top. We would sleep in the middle of one of the huge bushes, all huddled together and very afraid. During the day we would return to the house for a very short time to get something to eat and then go back and hide. Papa and the other men armed themselves with clubs and machetes and roamed around the area, trying to protect their families.

Nothing happened to us that day, but the stories we heard of what was going on elsewhere convinced us that it would not be long. It was clear that the lists about which we had heard actually did exist. Within hours of the President's death, the people whose names were on the lists began to be visited and slaughtered in their homes, including moderate Hutus who would have been against the mass killing of Tutsis. Bands of trained killers known as the Interahamwe led the way, often dressed in flamboyant yellow, red and green, but all Hutus were forced to join in. Those who refused to comply were threatened with death.

People fleeing from Kigali began to stream through our area, each face betraying its own story of abject terror. They told of people fleeing into churches, schools and hospitals for safety, only to be surrounded by hundreds of killers who threw hand grenades into the building before entering and setting upon their helpless victims with machetes, clubs, spades and any other tool they could find. Death was often not these killers' sole aim; their aim was to inflict death as cruelly as possible and so it was preceded by beatings, torture and mutilation, and for many, many women by brutal rape.

We were the "enemy." It was not long before the RTLM was broadcasting the blatant message, "Kill the cockroaches! Kill the snakes! Find those Tutsis wherever they are and kill them. Kill them all, the old, the young, men and women. Don't even be afraid of killing pregnant women. We need to rid our country of this evil." There was a song they used to play on the radio:

Umwanzi wacu n'umwe
turamuzi
n'umututsi.

Our enemy is one
We know him
It is the Tutsi.

With so many people coming to our area to try to escape, we began to wonder where we would go when our turn came. We were now in no doubt whatsoever that come it would.

A couple of days later Mama asked Papa to take the boys to the hairdresser's to get their hair cut. "I want them to look smart when they are killed," she said. She also packed some of our clothes in a suitcase and took them over to our neighbor Felecita's house, even though this old friend of the family had become increasingly hostile towards us. "Please could you keep these for me?" she asked. "If we survive, I will come back for them."

After a few days of sleeping in the woods, Régis was beginning to get very upset because he was so disturbed, frightened and overtired, and Mama decided to take him home in the hope that a decent night's sleep would help him cope better. She hadn't been home long when there was a great deal of shouting not far from the house and Mama's best friend Beatà, Claudette's mother, arrived at the house looking absolutely terrified. She told Mama that her husband had just been killed and her house had been set on fire, and pleaded with her to look after two of her boys, Bébé, who was five, and Olivier, who was four. She had taken her other five children somewhere safe but now she needed to go and find them. She went off, taking with her her one-year-old son Lambert.

After that Mama knew that she couldn't stay at the house and came straight back to the forest with the three children. The little four-year-old boy, Olivier, was in deep shock. He couldn't speak; he couldn't even cry. He didn't seem to understand what people were saying when they spoke to him. He wanted to be on my mother's back the whole time. We wondered if he had witnessed his father being murdered.

Mama had not been back long when Papa arrived, running. Never before had I seen him look the way he did. Quickly explaining that soldiers had arrived with guns and that, when they had started to shoot, everyone had scattered, he told us, "The only thing we can do is make a run for it." When I heard him say those words, I knew that we were not going to survive. Papa said to Mama, "Try to take the children to some of our neighbors. We haven't been bad neighbors. Perhaps they will hide them for a few days until we see what's going to happen." Then he shouted to the group of about thirty other people who were with us in the forest, "Run for your lives. They're coming. Just get out of here." Everyone started running in different directions. My mum, my brothers, my sister, the two boys and I started running towards the school for disabled children, but a Tutsi who came running from that direction shouted at us that they were already killing down there and burning houses. People were running here, there and everywhere, and we just didn't know what to do, so we ended up going back into the forest. All around us everyone was talking about the people they knew who had been killed.

Mama told my sister Mimi, my cousin Valérie, who had also been sleeping in the forest, and me to go to the house of one of our Hutu neighbors, Esily, and hide there, saying that she would come for us in the morning. "But Mama, he won't let us," I said. "If he doesn't," she said, "just run for your lives."

It was just beginning to get dark when we arrived at Esily's house. Normally a friendly and approachable man he glared at us with his hands on his hips and demanded, "What are you doing here?"

"Mama told us to come here," we said. "Things are terrible."

"I know things are terrible, but what have you come here for?"

"Mama asked if you would let us sleep here for tonight, and she will come and get us in the morning."

He laughed, probably thinking that she would not see another morning. "You can't sleep here," he said.

"Please," we pleaded, "just tonight. We'll go in the morning."

His wife intervened. "Just let them stay tonight. They can go tomorrow."

Even though one of their children had been in the same class as me at primary school, they did not let us sleep in the same room as their children, but they just got out a grass mat and laid it out on the floor, near the door. "You can sleep there," they said. They did not even give us a blanket, just another grass mat to cover ourselves with. We were freezing. We all three lay there, but I don't think any of us slept. Everything was going round and round in my head. What was happening to Mama and the boys? How was she going to manage to run with that little four-year-old boy? What had happened to Papa and my brothers? Were they safe somewhere? How could people change like that? And I thought about what it would be like to be killed with a machete. The night was very, very long – much too long. We did not dare to speak to one another; we just lay there, tormented by our thoughts.

The next day was a Saturday and Esily and his family were

Seventh Day Adventists. Esily's wife and children went to church – they had nothing to worry about because they were Hutus. Esily went out too, but we were not sure if he also went to church. They had not given us anything to eat or drink, and we were very hungry and thirsty.

Around mid-morning Esily arrived back. We could see he had been running. "You have to go now," he said.

"Please let us stay," we begged. "Where can we go?"

"No, you must go. They may come and search the house, and I don't want you to die here. You have to leave now."

We pleaded and pleaded with him to let us stay, saying that we did not know where our parents were or where we could go, but he was adamant. As we were leaving he said, "All the Tutsis are up on the mountain, so that they can see the killers coming. Go and join them."

We ran as quickly as we could to the small mountain covered with boulders behind the village which was known as Ruganzu Rocks. Two or three hundred Tutsis had gathered there. In the crowd I saw my mum's friend who was nine-months' pregnant. Some of the young men were holding machetes and stones but you could tell from the look on their faces that they weren't going to be able to use them. All hope had drained away from these people and they knew they were going to die. I found my three brothers but neither Mama nor Papa was there.

"Have you seen Mama?" I asked Régis.

"No, I don't know where she is. We got separated. Perhaps she's been killed."

People did not seem to realize that although they had fled to the mountain so they could see the killers coming, they were also making it easier for the killers to find them. Children were crying; the elderly were stunned into silence, knowing that when the time came they would be too weak to run. I tried to keep hold of Régis' hand, but he kept tearing it away from me.

A little while later Régis screamed, "The killers are coming. The killers are coming." He had seen the sunshine glinting on the brand-new machetes the government had supplied them with. There were hundreds of them. As they marched towards us they were singing their disgusting song, "Kill them all. Kill the babies, kill the mothers, kill the young ones, kill the old ones . . . " In front of the killers marched a line of government soldiers carrying guns, who had been sent into the area to mobilize the local Hutus. They were ready to deal with any Tutsis brave enough to put up any resistance.

Suddenly shots were fired and panic erupted. There was a stampede as people started running in all directions. We joined a group of people fleeing towards another mountain where they hoped to be able to hide in the forest. As we approached it we saw that the way was impeded by soldiers firing into the air to scare people, so we all turned round and ran back the way we had come. In the confusion my sister and I lost sight of my brothers. After a while we came across my grandmother and my two aunts, Martha and Mary. They were carrying my two little cousins, Clare (4) and Uwera (5), who had been staying with them for the school holidays.

We ran and ran. We were trying to get to the primary school where we thought we might be able to shelter, but as we made our way down the valley towards the school we saw a group of killers slaughtering people with their machetes. We changed direction and tried the headmaster's house, but it was locked and everyone had left. We were all exhausted. Then my grandmother made a decision. "We'll go home," she said, "and we'll die there."

"We can't go home, Grandma," I said. "We'll be killed if we go home."

"We'll be killed wherever we go," she replied. "It's happening all over the country. Nowhere is safe. We'll have to go home."

After she said that, I just shut up.

We started walking in the direction of home. We had barely walked ten steps when we saw a young man being chased by some killers with their machetes. As they ran, they were blowing whistles to alert other killers of their prey. The piercing sound almost paralyzed me. Others were still singing as they chased him. We quickly hid ourselves in a bush and kept very quiet, listening in silent horror as the machetes sliced into his body. The boy was so terrified that he was not even able to utter one scream. When they had finished him off, they threw his body into a nearby ditch, which had been dug to collect water in the rainy season, and went on their way.

Not far from home we saw a Hutu man holding a machete standing near his house. He kept watching us and seemed to be trying to warn us not to go any further. A few moments later we could see why. Further down the road there was another Hutu who was searching for people to kill. As soon as he had gone, the first man came over to us. He recognized my grandmother and asked her if she was Stephan's wife. When she said she was, he asked where we were going. Hearing that we were on our way home, he exclaimed, "No, you can't go there. They've been searching for you. If you go there, you'll be killed."

"We don't know what else to do," my grandmother said. "Can you hide us?"

"No," he said. "I would love to but I can't. In the meeting they said they would kill any Hutu they found helping Tutsis."

We had no choice but to walk on towards our home. The familiar tracks were eerily quiet. As we made our way through the cypress woods, there was no way of knowing who was lurking in the shadows. The atmosphere was very heavy, laden with fear. All the Hutus were out looking for people to kill. They had set up roadblocks everywhere. Back on the mountain I had heard story after story of what the killers were using these roadblocks for. They were calling them "killing centers" where they herded people to kill them, gang-raping the women before brutally murdering them. Sometimes they made people wait for hours before killing them. The bodies of the people they killed were thrown, where possible, into the communal latrines (huge pits with planks across them, enclosed by brick walls) or, if these were already full, into large trenches dug for the purpose – anywhere they could find to stop the dogs getting hold of them.

Then we met Kabayiza, who was the son of our neighbor Felecita and used to work in our plantation. He was the young man to whom my father had loaned one of our cows so that his baby could have fresh milk every day, later giving him the cow's calf to keep. Seeing he was carrying a machete, we backed away, fearing the worst.

"Kabayiza," I said, "you can't be killing too?"

"No," he replied. "I've been searching for you everywhere. Your mother asked me to try and find you."

"You mean she's still alive?" I asked.

"Yes, she's still alive. She's hiding with your brothers."

"Can you take us to her?"

"No, I can't take you to where she is, but I'll take you to my house for a few hours and then we'll decide what to do."

He took us to his small house, next to his mother's, and hid all seven of us under his very small bed. His wife was away at the time visiting her family. He told us, "Don't say a word. If you hear anyone knock on the door, just stay where you are.

Don't try to run away. Since I'm a Hutu no one can enter my house without my permission, I'm going to go and see what's happening."

We were all totally exhausted. We had been on the run since early morning without having anything to eat or drink. Kabayiza had left us a few sweet potatoes, but it was only enough to feed my two young cousins. We found some water in a small pot. It was very dirty but we were so thirsty we drank it. As we lay under the bed, sweating in the heat, we could hear loud bangs coming from our house further up the valley. When Kabayiza returned home, he told us what the banging was. "They've just finished completely destroying your home. The cows have gone, all the animals ... they've taken your clothes ... everything. They suspect me of hiding your father and they're coming here later to search the house. You'll have to get out of here."

"Where can we go now?" we asked. "We've nowhere to go."

"I've spoken to Simon, and he says you can go there until we decide what to do."

Simon was another of our neighbors.

"Is everyone killing?" I asked him.

"Yes," he answered, "everyone is joining in the killing."

"Even Jason and Munyentwari's sons?"

"Yes," he said.

I could not believe that these people whom I had trusted and my parents had helped so much, had become killers.

As we crept through a hole in the wall of Kabayiza's house past his mother's tiny house, I could see our roof tiles piled up on the floor inside.

"Where did you get these?" I asked Felecita.

"I didn't steal them," she said. "I was given them. Anyone can take anything they like from your house now."

I couldn't believe it. Felecita was a Catholic. She had been in our house almost every day since I was born. Now she was stealing our things.

Kabayiza left us hiding in the banana plantation. He did not want to move us until the middle of the night. Even then it was very dangerous as the killers hardly slept but kept searching through the villages looking for more Tutsis to kill. The more they killed, it seemed, the more thirsty they became for blood. As we waited, we could hear them come to search Kabayiza's house. "I want to find those young girls of Bernard's," one man said. "I'm going to rape them before I kill them – especially that proud one." He was referring to my sister Mimi. The search of the small house did not take long. "I told you they're not here," Kabayiza told them when they came out. "Let's go and get a drink."

It was another couple of hours before he came back, and by then it was one or two o'clock in the morning. He told us: "They're convinced that I know where you are. I'm sure they'll come back. I need to get you away from here. Now listen: I'm going to go ahead of you. Watch me and I'll signal to you when the way is clear." By this time my two little cousins had fallen fast asleep.

Keeping our eyes on Kabiyaza and watching for his signal, we crept along the hill. Crouching very low under the banana trees and cassava bushes, trying to make as little sound as we could, it seemed a very long way, although in reality it wasn't that far. When we reached Simon's house he was waiting anxiously outside. We were not allowed to go straight in, but we each had to wait until he was sure the coast was clear and then he signaled to us one at a time that we could run in. Just before I took my leave of Kabayiza, I begged him, "Please, if you see Mama or any of my brothers, can you tell them that I love them and that if we should die, we'll meet again in heaven. And please, if you can, find out if Papa is still alive."

Once again all seven of us were told to hide under the bed. On top of the wooden bed his two children were sleeping on several layers of banana leaves. Warning us not to say a word, Simon told us that he would leave the fire burning so that passers-by would think that his wife was inside. In fact he and his wife were having problems and she had gone back to live with her parents. He locked the door and went to sit outside so that he could see what was going on. Several times, as I lay awake under the bed, crushed between my sister and my auntie, in the pitch darkness, I heard men shouting to him that they were on their way to kill someone and he should come with them. "Yeah, I'm with you. I'm with you. I'll be right after you," he shouted back.

We had arrived at his house early Sunday morning and we stayed there for three days. During that time Simon was often drunk, and we were all constantly afraid and very surprised that he did not let slip that we were there in his house. The house was sweltering hot because he kept the fire on all day and the atmosphere was very smoky, but we dare not cough or make a sound. Now and again he would give us something to eat. We tried not to drink too much because we could only go to the toilet late at night, when Simon would take us all one by one to the outside toilet, being very careful to ensure that we were not seen. From time to time the two little children would understandably get upset and start saying that they wanted to go home or that they wanted their mum or their dad. Then we would try every means possible to get them to be quiet again. After several days of lying under the bed in the dark, one night when I crawled out I could not see anything. I burst into tears and wailed, "I'm blind! I'm blind! I can't see anything." My aunt comforted me, "Don't worry. It's just because you've been lying in the dark for so long."

On Tuesday Kabayiza came back, bringing the news that Mama and Beatà's children were safe and so were my brothers. He came to tell Simon that Alestide and Kiki could no longer stay at their hiding place and so he was going to bring them to where we were. After that there were nine of us, all hiding under the one small bed. From what the men said, the Hutus were hunting high and low for my brothers and had a strong suspicion that Kabayiza and Simon were protecting them. These two men did all they could to help us.

When Kiki arrived, he was very sick with malaria. The two boys had no news of my mother. I asked Simon for a piece of paper and a pen to write a note which I hoped Kabayiza could take to her. He had to hunt high and low to find one, but he eventually came up with a dog-eared scrap. I wrote, "Mama, I don't know whether you will survive or whether I will survive. I don't feel as if I will survive, but if you survive, remember that I love you." Mama managed to get a note through to Grandma which said, "Just be strong and know that God is with us. If we die, we will die in His arms."

Kiki and Alestide only stayed at the house for a short while before being taken to another hiding place. We kept asking Simon if there was any news of my father. One day he came back saying that he had heard my father was alive. A day or so later our hopes were crushed when he told us our father was dead. I began to cry, but my grandmother said to me, "This is no time to cry. Don't cry for the dead. Cry for the living." So we all held our tears. In fact, my father was not yet dead.

After three days Simon announced, "It's safe for you to go now. From now on they're only going to kill men and boys, so it's safe for you women to go back home."

My grandmother was immediately alarmed. "What do you mean, 'It's safe'?" How can you say we are safe when these people have killed our husbands, they have killed our sons, they have killed our brothers? How can you say that they are going to have mercy on us after they have done all that? It's a lie. You want to expose us so that we will all be killed."

He retorted, "If you don't go, I will go and call them and tell them to come and get you. You have to go now – I don't want you to die here."

With great dignity, my grandmother turned to us and said, "Come, we'll go to Grandfather's house and wait there for our death."

Chapter 5

WAITING FOR DEATH

All that was left of my grandparents' house was a shell. The roof was gone and so were the windows and doors. Everything had been taken apart from my grandfather's books, which lay strewn across the floor. Sitting in the midst of the desolation was my grandfather. He looked very thin and full of despair. He had thought we were all already dead. Although he was glad to see us, his face remained emotionless. After we had embraced him, he told us that time and time again he had been taken to the killing center to be killed, but each time they had brought him back again. Because he was such a respected member of the community, they kept saying that they were going to leave him till the end. From what he had seen he was the only Tutsi man left alive.

For the next four days we waited for death. The Hutus knew we were there, but they also knew we wouldn't be going anywhere. During those days we had very little to eat or drink but, since it was the rainy season, we drank the water we collected on banana leaves or in our cupped hands. When he could, our grandfather's herdsman Martin brought us milk from his cows. When there was no one around, we would creep into the surrounding plantations and gather any vegetables we could find, cooking them in an old broken pot. So often the meager meals we were able to cook were just heartlessly tipped onto the ground by any Hutu killer who happened to be passing at that moment.

On the second day we were joined by my father's two cousins who arrived in a dreadful state – they could barely walk. As soon as they saw us, they collapsed in floods of tears. They told us that they had been raped over and over again by different killers. Asumpta was twenty-one and Fifi was nineteen.

On the third day – Tuesday – Mama arrived with Beatà's two boys. The message we had heard from Simon that the women were no longer going to be killed had been put around the whole village and so all the women and their children were emerging from their hiding places. Somehow Mama had found out that we were all together at Grand-father's house and had come to join us there. She was absolutely exhausted. The three of them had been hiding at the home of Rwubusisi, one of our neighbors who was an old friend of the family. Mama was godmother to one of his children.

In the middle of that night we were all scared out of our wits by a man dropping down into the house from the roof. This man no longer looked human. He had the face of a man who was utterly terrified. So many people had died that I thought it must be a ghost, but gradually we realized it was my father. We were amazed that he was still alive but shocked by what we saw. He looked terrible. He had lost so much weight; his hair was long and unkempt, and he had grown a beard; his clothes were filthy and he had no shoes. He too had been in hiding, we discovered, but having been sent away by his protector, he had been hiding among the rooftops – they were often overhung by banana trees and their broad leaves provided secluded hiding places. He stayed with us for the rest of the night but then he left. Since they were saying that the women were no longer going to be killed, he thought we would be safer if he was not there. He continued to hide among the rooftops, watching us from a distance.

The next day Mama asked Kabayiza to go and fetch my brothers so that we could all be together. From somewhere she found some dresses and told the boys to put them on. Of course they complained like mad, but she made them do it. There was the faintest glimmer of hope that what they were saying was true, but in our heart of hearts we knew that the killing was not going to stop. There were now sixteen of us, waiting together.

That same afternoon the killers came for us. It was Wednesday 4 May. We heard their songs before we saw them. They were a disgusting sight. Vying with each other for the reputation of the fiercest killer they would use banana leaves to strap the hands of their victims around their head or around their wrists. Many of them would also drink human blood.

As we were herded out of the house and onto the street, we met fifty or sixty other women and children who had also been rounded up. Among them were some boys who, like my brothers, had been forced by their mothers to wear dresses. We were being taken to the roadblock they were using as a killing center, about a ten-minute walk away.

Brandishing his Bible in the air, my grandfather, who was the only man among the crowd, went to the head of the desolate column of people with us following close behind him. "Sing," he urged everyone. "Sing, because this is the last time you're going to sing. They may kill our bodies, but they can never kill our spirits. We're going to heaven!" Then he started up a rousing hymn, and many people joined in. While with my mouth I was forming the words, in my heart I was screaming out to God, "Why have You abandoned us, God? Why are You allowing these people to do this to us?" As far as I was concerned God had stopped listening.

We had only gone a short way when the killers halted the crowd of people. They said to a fourteen-year-old youth carrying a blood-stained machete, "We haven't eaten yet today and we're hungry. You take this lot to the killing center while we go and get something to eat. We'll meet you there later. They won't go anywhere." This boy had been in the same primary-school class as me. Seventy or eighty people allowed this fourteen-year-old boy to lead them to their death. We were weak from hunger and exhaustion. We were in despair. We had nowhere to run.

When we reached the killing center my heart almost stopped. There was blood everywhere. Several hundred women and children were already there. We sat down with all the others and waited for death.

When the killers came back, they talked among themselves about how they were going to kill so many people and then dispose of their bodies.

"We're going to need a grenade to finish all these people off," one said. "It'll take too long to kill them all."

"What are you talking about?" another man said. "Killing Tutsis isn't hard work," and with that he began to hit out at a woman who was sitting right next to me and she fell over on top of me. I really thought that my moment to die had come.

"Stop it! Stop it!" another man intervened. "We can't kill them yet. There are too many of them. We have no way of getting rid of their bodies. You know, those Tutsis smell so bad. We need to get hold of a grenade first."

"A grenade?" the man who wanted to get on with it argued. "Tutsis don't deserve grenades or bullets. Have they paid for them?" Then turning to the crowd, he shouted, "If any of you Tutsis has money, come forward. If you pay us 5,000 Francs[2] we will shoot you, instead of killing you with a machete."

But no one had any money. After that the leader of the killers told us to go away, saying they would kill us another day. "They are ours," he told his group of men. "We can have them anytime we want."

When we got back to the house we were all starving hungry. Before they had taken us, my grandmother had cooked some vegetables which she had tried to hide. By the time we got back, they had gone. We were so hungry that we chewed on banana leaves.

A day later, on the Friday, a woman came to the house to gloat over us. She was a Tutsi but she was married to a Hutu and her sons were very heavily involved in the killing. She said all sorts of insulting things to my grandmother and made horrible threats about what the Hutus were going to do to us. My grandmother said to her, "Today it is us; tomorrow it may be you."

Later the same day one of Kiki's friends who was a Hutu came to the house. He was very agitated. He had just come from a meeting held by the killers. The following day, 7 May, the assassinated Hutu president was due to be buried and the killers, wanting to mark the occasion, were intending to kill all the remaining Tutsi women and children on the day. Their blood was to be "a cover" for the president's grave. Asking that we didn't tell anyone that it was he who had told us of the Hutus' plan, he begged, "They're coming to kill you tomorrow. You've got to make a run for it." When he had

2. About £5 – beyond the reach of most Rwandans.

gone, Kiki wanted to try to escape, but my grandfather persuaded him against it. "There's nowhere to run. If you try to escape they will certainly kill you. Stay here, and let's die together. At least then we will all be buried together."

The hours dragged slowly by, with few words being exchanged between us. Physically, mentally and emotionally exhausted, we were all in an extremely traumatized state – already more dead than alive. Only Kiki, with the resources of his youth, tried to break the tension with the occasional joke. Knowing that my grandmother had dug up some cassava, he urged her to cook it, saying, "Let me eat today because tomorrow I won't be able to." I sometimes wonder why we didn't run away, but I think it was because death was already in our heads.

That night as a family we all huddled together in the pitch darkness in the tiny, now roofless storeroom of Grandfather's house. Led by Grandfather, we knelt together and repented of our sins before God. Knowing that we were to die the next day, we could not sleep. We just waited for death.

In a corner of my heart there was still a vestige of hope that by some miracle we might be saved. We had heard somehow that the Tutsi fighters were advancing and that they had saved some people in Kigali. As we sat waiting in the small hours of the night I said to my mother, "Do you think that a miracle might happen and the Tutsi fighters might come and rescue us?"

"Don't talk to me about those stupid fighters," she said angrily. "They are the ones to blame for all this trouble. They brought this upon us and they can't even finish what they started."

"Mama," I said, "don't speak against them. They might still come and save us."

Very early the next morning, about 3 o'clock, we suddenly

heard a great deal of noise and commotion coming from our nearest neighbors' house, twenty or thirty meters away. There was a family with young children living there, as well as a woman who was nine-months' pregnant. She was the one I had seen on the mountain when we were trying to escape. The babies and young children were screaming with terror. There were the sounds of clubs crashing down on people's heads and machetes slicing into their bodies. I heard one child cry out, "Please forgive me. Please forgive me. I promise I will never be a Tutsi again." Gradually the screams subsided as one by one they were all murdered. We heard the dull thud as each body was thrown into the toilet of the house and the door slammed shut. The pregnant woman was obviously not yet dead and we heard her moans. After a few minutes, silence. Shaken to the core with the horror of what we had heard, we huddled together. Trembling. Terrified.

Next they came to us.

First came a young man. He was covered in blood and the machete in his hand was still dripping with blood. We recognized him. He had been in the football team Papa had formed for my brothers and the local lads in the area. He looked at us. Then he turned round and went back to the other killers who had surrounded the house. "There's no one here," he told them. "They've all gone."

Then the leader of the killers came into the house and saw us. His name was Gakuba. He was an elder in the Seventh Day Adventist church. When we saw him, we all immediately covered our faces with our hands. The sight of him was horrifying. So full of blood. So much evil in his eyes. So much hatred. "So they are not here, are they? You say you didn't see all these snakes cowering in here?"

"No, I didn't see them. It's too dark in here to see." The young man tried to sound convincing.

"Well, if you want to make up for your little mistake, you'd better kill at least ten of them."

"I will, I will," the young man stuttered. "But I tell you I didn't see them."

"Outside!" he ordered us.

My grandfather got up and we all followed, keeping as close to him as we could. Now we had to face our killers.

My grandfather had his Bible in his hands. He fell to his knees and began to implore the men for mercy. "Why are you killing us? We have lived side by side with you as your brothers and sisters. What have we done? I taught you as I taught my own children. Jesus Christ told us that we should love one another. Why are you condemning yourselves by having our blood on your hands? Why don't you just forgive us?"

On and on he went, begging them, pleading with them. Finally Gakuba said, "Stop wasting our time, old man. We've got too much work to do today." Then turning to one of his men, he said, "Check the toilet and see how much room there is in there." The man came back saying that it was already full.[3]

Again my grandfather cried out, "Why can't you forgive us?"

"We will spare you and your wife, because you are old," Gakuba relented. "But all the rest of these snakes will have to die. But be quick and make up your mind. You are wasting our time."

"If you kill my children and my grandchildren, what is the point of me living?" my grandfather said. "What is the use of a tree without its branches? I choose to die with my children and my grandchildren."

3. I do not know how these bodies came to be there, but it is possible that they were the corpses of people fleeing through the area who had been murdered by local killers.

Then he asked that we be allowed to pray together for the last time. "What's the point?" they said. "You Tutsis have no God. God has forsaken you." But they let him have his wish. We all knelt together as he prayed. Before he had even finished, some of the men grabbed hold of my mother and started tearing at her clothes, ready to rape her. The little four-year-old was on her back.

"Why are you raping me in front of my children?" she screamed. "Kill them first so that at least they do not have to witness that, and then you can do whatever you like to me." She did not want us to suffer any more than we were already suffering.

"If that's the way you want it," said Gakuba.

At that moment one of the killers came back and told them that they had found a place to dump our bodies. They took us a short distance from the house where, on the edge of my grandparents' banana plantation, there was a long, thin trench about a meter deep, in which rain water had begun to collect. We were ordered into the pit and then Gakuba shouted, "Now choose which weapon you want to kill you! And hurry up. We have got so much to do today."

As I looked up at the twenty or more killers crowding around the edge of the trench, in my head I was screaming out, "This can't be happening! I know you. You are my neighbors. You can't be about to kill us." I looked at the terrifying weapons they were carrying. There were machetes, knives, spears, clubs, spades and sticks studded with nails. They were all already drenched in blood. It was the machetes and the knives I most feared. I had seen people killed with clubs – they hit them once or twice on the back of the head, the brains came out, and it was all over. I knew one of the men carrying a club – he was a young man called John.

I heard my mother say, "Death is death. I will not choose."

I said, "I choose John. Please don't kill me with anything else."

All the young children were crying, but the rest of us were silent. That moment was beyond any emotion.

We were all told to lie face-down on the bottom of the trench. It was not wide enough to lie across it, so we all had to lie lengthwise, our bodies overlapping each other in the confined space. Just as my grandfather was saying again, "Why don't you forgive us?" he was hit with a stick by Gatoya, one of the men who had wanted to rape my mother, and he fell forward. As I looked across at my mother I saw a machete coming down onto her neck and her head falling to the side. Then I saw them cut off her leg. She made no sound. I heard my brothers cry out, "Please forgive me, please forgive me" and then scream with searing pain. I put my hands over my face. At that moment the club hit me. My tongue came out of my mouth and I could feel blood pouring down my chin. Then I was plunged into unconsciousness.

I don't know how long I was unconscious for. When I came round again, I heard the killers talking. They were talking and joking about how long it took Tutsis to die, even the old and the very young. They were stepping over the bodies, looking to see if anyone was still alive. Of course, they were piled on top of one another and it was not easy for them to see. My little cousin was lying next to me. I could hear her moaning gently. "This one's not dead yet," a man standing over her shouted. Thud. His weapon came down on her and her blood splattered over me. Then I heard John's voice. "I'm going to cut these feet off," he said. The feet he was talking about were mine. A moment later I felt excruciating pain but I did not move a muscle or make a sound. I did not even take a breath. He did not take the whole foot off but just slashed the back of both my heels. They were working in a hurry because they wanted to move on. When they thought that everyone was dead, they filled in the trench again, so that the bodies were covered with a thick layer of earth, and went away. I did not know at the time that my father had watched his whole family being killed.

Chapter 6

"You Will Suffer but You Will Live"

I was lying face down in mud and blood. Many people have asked me how I survived but I tell them I do not know. The only answer I can give is that God saved me. I know that my Aunt Martha was also buried alive. My head was lying on her side, and I could hear her groans and feel her body convulsing. I called to her but there was no response. Then the groans stopped and I knew she had died. She only survived a few minutes. But I lay there entombed for something like thirteen or fourteen hours.

I could not move. The earth pressed heavily on my body. The smell of blood filled my nostrils and the taste of blood filled my mouth. As the hours passed, an intense cold crept over me. I tried to shout for help but no sound seemed to come out of my mouth. As I lay there in the pitch blackness, with the dead bodies of my loved ones all around me, I prayed, "Lord, if You take me out of this grave, I will serve You all the days of my life and I will be a nun."

The hours passed, but death did not come. It must have

been about three or four in the afternoon when I felt a pressure on the ground above my head. Someone must have been walking over the filled-in trench. Then they stood still. Summoning every remaining ounce of energy in my body, I tried to shout for one last time.

After a few seconds the person moved off. Or perhaps it was a stray dog which could smell the bodies.

Minutes later though, I heard voices and the sound of digging. At first they dug in the wrong place and found only a corpse, but they persisted and eventually they found me. Digging with their spades, they uncovered the top part of my body. My rescuers were two Hutus, Lambert and Nshokeye. Lambert was a young man of nineteen who used to work for my grandfather. He had come to our grave, knowing that someone might still be alive. It was well known that sometimes the Hutu killers deliberately buried people alive to make their death even more horrific. Lambert really loved my grandfather and the whole family. He had consistently refused to have any part in the killing of the Tutsis, despite having been threatened, beaten and attacked with machetes by his fellow Hutus. As a result he walked with a limp. He had heard the shout which I was not even sure had come out of my mouth and had run to fetch the other man. Nshokeye was the son of the Tutsi woman who – can it have really just been two days before? – had come to gloat over our family. Perhaps Lambert thought that because Nshokeye had a Tutsi mother he would show some mercy to the poor wretch that had managed to cheat death. He was wrong, however. Seeing I was indeed still alive, Nshokeye reached for his machete, intending to cut off my head.

"Kill me," I said. "Go ahead and kill me. I want to die."

As Nshokeye raised his machete, Lambert rammed his whole body against him and threatened, "Up till now I haven't killed anyone, but if you touch her, I swear I will kill you!"

"She is asking to die," the other man said.

"Leave her," Lambert warned, his voice bristling with rage.

Seeing that he was in deadly earnest, Nshokeye let his machete fall to his side. The two men then tried to drag me out of the earth by my arms. I thought my body was going to be torn in two. I was covered in blood and mud – my eyes, my nose, my hair, everything ... Congealed blood covered the wound at the back of my head and the gashes on my heels. My head was swollen.

As the earth finally released my body, I ended up in the arms of Nshokeye. At that very moment there was the sound of singing and shouting and a roaming band of Hutu killers came into view. These men were not from the area and had a reputation of being even more vicious than the local killers. They never showed any mercy. "Shh, keep quiet," Nshokeye hissed, throwing me down on the mound of earth they had created with their digging. The two men ran off, warning, "Don't ever tell anyone who rescued you."

The five killers surveyed my crumpled, filthy, bloodied body. "What are you? Are you a human being or a ghost?" asked one killer, who wore the hands of his victims displayed as trophies around his head.

I wiped the mud from my eyes and said, "I am a human being." I was not afraid any more.

"Are you a human being or a ghost?" another demanded.

"I am a human being," I repeated.

They asked the question again and again, hardly able to believe the answer I was giving them. Witchcraft was so much a part of their way of life that they could well believe that I was the spirit of one of their victims. Then they wanted to know where I had come from. When I told them I had come out of the trench a few meters away, they asked me who had dug me out.

"I dug myself out," I told them.

"Finish her off," the leader ordered.

"Yes, kill me," I said. "I want to die."

"You are already dead," they kept saying.

None of the men wanted to kill me, each saying that he did not kill ghosts. While the killers stood talking, deliberating among themselves whether I was a ghost or a human being, I caught a snatch of a conversation between some men a short distance away. What I heard devastated me. One man said, "Have you heard what happened this morning?"

"No, what happened?" came the reply.

"We killed Bernard. All this time he was hiding up on the roof of his father's house."

All hope that my father was still alive was finally extinguished. All hope that I might see him again one day was obliterated. As the killers turned to leave, saying, "Just leave her to die. She'll be dead in twenty minutes," I pleaded with them again, "Are you going without killing me? Just kill me, I want to die." They just laughed and went on their way.

As soon as they were out of sight, Lambert, who had been watching from a distance, came over to me, bringing me a cup of milk. "Thank God you're still alive," he said. "I felt sure they would kill you." He told me that a woman called Nirere, who lived nearby, had agreed to take me for the night. She had three young children, two boys and a girl. He went a short way ahead to make sure the coast was clear and motioned for me to follow. I tried to stand but I immediately collapsed back onto the ground. Lambert put me over his shoulder and carried me to Nirere's house.

When Nirere saw me, she burst into tears. "Frida, what have they done to you? What have they done? What has become of us Hutus? We are like animals! We are bringing a curse on our nation."

I was too weak and exhausted to speak. She hid me under an enormous stack of bean plants that she had drying in her tiny house. I could hear rats moving about. Normally I would have been terrified, but now I was past caring about anything.

Soon after Lambert left, saying that he would come back in the morning. Unbeknown to us, we had been seen entering Nirere's house. Moments later four killers came into the house, demanding that she hand me over to them. She vehemently denied any knowledge of me, saying, "You know I hate Tutsis. And if I wasn't able to save her grandfather Stephan, whom I worked for and who was my good neighbor for so many years, what chance would I have of saving her?"

Refusing to take her word for it, they demanded to search the house, threatening that if they found me, they would kill her and her children.

"Go ahead," she said, "but you won't find her."

I could hear them rattling and banging as they searched through the house. Not finding me, they pounced upon the huge pile of bean plants. Angrily they plunged their spears into the stack. With each thrust of their spear they shouted out, "You mean she's not in here?", "She's not in here?" I did not move a muscle. Amazingly, no spear touched me.

They were convinced I was in that house somewhere and refused to give up. They were starting to dismantle the pile, angrily tossing the plants all over the floor of the house, when one of their leaders came to find them. "What are you doing wasting your time looking for that girl?" he shouted. "Don't you realize that those Tutsi rebels, those cockroaches, are advancing towards this area? If we don't finish off the rest of those Tutsis today, it will be too late. Stop wasting time. Come on."

"We'll be back," they warned Nirere as they reluctantly left.

Fearing for the safety of her children, as soon as they had gone far enough, she sent me away.

Not knowing where I could go, desperately weak and hardly able to walk, I sat down on the ground a short distance from her house. Seeing me there, she came out and shouted at me, "Get right away from here. If they catch you anywhere near here, they will come and kill my children and me. Go away."

Each step was excruciatingly painful, but I got as far away from the house as I could. The whole of that night I lay by the edge of a banana plantation. I did not care whether I lived or died. I did not sleep. I just lay there, listening to the never-ending shouts of the killers whose appetite for blood was still not satisfied. I don't know how it found me, but my father's dog Bobby came and lay by my side as if it was trying to protect me.

Early the next morning I realized that I was too exposed and that I needed to find somewhere to hide. Remembering how Mama had hidden us all in the bushes I found a huge bush and crept underneath it. The dog was still following me. I tried to chase it away but it would not leave me. A couple of hours later the bush was surrounded by people. The word had got round that I had survived – probably Nshokeye had been talking – and my survival was adding fire to a worry that was growing among the Hutu killers. With the increasing pressure of the impending arrival of the Tutsi fighters, they were beginning to fear reprisals. They were well aware that any surviving Tutsis would be able to tell the story of their atrocities. "These people who aren't being finished off properly," they were saying to one another, "are the very ones who will tell the Tutsi cockroaches what we have done. We have got to find them and kill them so they can't talk."

Noticing that my father's dog was staying close to one particular bush, they put two and two together and realized I was in there.

The dog was making a terrible noise barking at them all. "If you don't come out," they shouted, "we'll set fire to the bush and you'll burn to death." I didn't really care if they set fire to the bush. To me burning to death seemed preferable to being attacked with a machete or knife. But, as they were shouting, they were thrusting their machetes and their sticks into the bush and they were gradually getting closer and closer to me. My fear of machetes forced me out of the bush. When I emerged they could not believe they had expended so much effort looking for such a pitiful creature. "You mean we've spent all this time looking for this wretched girl?" they said to one another. "She's half dead already. Just leave her to die." Warning the people who lived in the area not to give me anything to eat or drink, they left me.

Just by the bush there was a large rock. I sat myself on the rock and waited. There was no point in trying to hide – everyone knew where I was. Again and again, as I sat there – alone and exposed for all the world to see – the realization that I was never going to see my family again hit me. My brain refused to take it in. I kept hoping I would wake up and realize it was just a horrible nightmare. There were no tears. There was no pain. I was too numb for that. There was just a huge chasm opening up inside me. As I sat there grappling with reality, one thought kept going round and round in my head: "You will suffer but you will live ... You will suffer but you will live ..." I tried to dismiss it. It was a crazy thought. How could I survive? I was all alone in the world. The Hutus were still hell bent on wiping the Tutsis off the face of the earth. My whole family was dead, and I wanted to die too. Nevertheless, the thought would not leave me.

After about half an hour a tall, thin man carrying a machete and a big bag came over to me. I recognized him as a neighbor of ours, whose smallholding lay on the opposite side of the valley. His face was very distinctive as one of his eyes was permanently half-shut. His name was Vitale. He said, "Come with me. I'm going to take you to my house. I'll carry you in this bag so that no one will see you." I did not trust him. I thought he was going to take me somewhere and rape me. But, perhaps swayed by the voice that was telling me I was going to survive, I went with him. And anyway, what option did I have? I refused point blank, however, to be put in the bag, fearing that I would suffocate inside it. Instead he found a small tree for me to hide behind. So now, half dead, I was being asked to carry a tree.

Vitale had already spoken with Nirere, the woman who had hidden me for a few hours the previous day, and she gave me some of her clothes to put over me. When we arrived at his house, his grown-up son was there. He was absolutely furious with his father for endangering the family's lives by taking me to their home and threatened to kill me. His father told him that if he laid a hand on me, he would kill him.

Vitale told me that I could stay at his home but that he would have to tell the men in charge that I was there – otherwise they would kill him. Then we would just have to wait and see what happened. Seeing the despair on my face, he tried to comfort me by saying, "Don't give up hope. You're not completely alone. Your grandfather's brother is still alive. They beat him unconscious and they intended to bury him alive, but while they were looking for somewhere to put him, someone stole his body. My brother has been hiding him at his house. It's going to be over soon. You might still come out of this alive." I told him, "Even if I live, I will have no hope, because all my family is dead."

For the next six weeks I remained in hiding at Vitale's house. During the day I would hide in the house. Knowing that the house might be searched at any time, at night he would hide me outside in his banana plantation, often changing the hiding place. Most of the time I slept in a small hole in the ground which he had dug. Once I was inside he would cover it with banana leaves and no one would ever have known there was a human being inside. Lying in the hole for hours on end my ears were deafened by the sound of my heart beating. When someone eventually came to fetch me, my legs were so numb that I could hardly walk.

One night while I was enclosed in my hidey-hole, I heard a dog nearby and there was a terrible smell. When I removed a few of the banana leaves to see what was causing the smell, I was horrified by what I saw. The dog was gnawing at my grandfather's arm. I could recognize his watch and the jacket he was wearing when he died.

I never knew whether Vitale had actually told the Hutu killers that he was sheltering me, but they never stopped looking for me and there were a couple of close shaves. On one occasion a very persistent man from the Batwa tribe called Ngamije came to the house. Rwandans always used to joke that these people, who made up only one percent of the nation, would blow with the wind as far as their allegiance was concerned. This man had been promised that he would be promoted to the rank of major in the army if he filled a very large pit right by the primary school for disabled children with the bodies of Tutsi women and girls, and he was determined to do it.

He came to Vitale's house during the day but for some reason I was hiding in my tiny hole in the banana plantation. He spent the whole day searching, first the house and then the plantation. Totally frustrated he was wildly chopping down banana leaves and these were falling over my hiding place, making it even more secure. I could see him through the leaves. At one point he climbed an avocado tree to try and get a better vantage point, but to no avail. Eventually, at about three in the afternoon, he gave up and went away.

On another occasion they came unexpectedly in the middle of the night to search the house and, unusually, I was sleeping inside. Vitale was very angry that he had not been warned that they were coming and at first he tried to stop them entering the house. When they demanded to be allowed to search, he insisted that I had already been apprehended and killed, but they were having none of it. Pushing past him, they began to search the house. His two daughters pulled me down on the floor where they were sleeping on banana leaves and lay on top of me, pulling the cover over them. One of the men pulled the cover down and shone a torch into their faces, but he did not see me.

I do not know why Vitale was so kind to me. Perhaps he was using me as a sort of insurance policy in case things ever went the other way. After I had been at his house for a while he also took in a young Tutsi man called Gaston who had somehow managed to survive. I have since come to understand that, at the same time that he was sheltering me, he was still going out every night with his machete to kill Tutsis. I only knew that, on his return, he would always wash his machete before he came into the house and spoke to me.

I had two visitors at Vitale's house. The first was Nirere, the woman who had sheltered me for a short time. After I had been there a week or two, she came to ask where my father kept the second-hand clothes he used to supply to the market-traders in Nyanza and where his "other treasures" were (by that she meant money). I did not know and I would not have told her anyway.

The second visitor was much more welcome. It was Lambert who had saved me. He came to see me several times. I told him about the voice I had heard in my head telling me over and over again, "You will suffer but you will live." After the genocide was over, he wrote me a letter in which he told me that he had felt like an angel when he had rescued me. He could not understand how I could have been buried in that grave for so many hours and yet survive. Although he was not a believer, he wrote, "I always wonder why God saved your life and what purpose He has for you."

Chapter 7

FACING LIFE ALONE

On 4 July the RPF took Kigali. The government fell and the tide in Rwanda turned. Bombs began to fall over Nyanza as the Tutsi forces drew nearer. I could not contain my joy that I was going to be saved, and this made Vitale's daughter very angry. She urged her father to kill me. "If you don't kill her," she said, "she will betray us all to the Tutsis." Vitale refused, saying, "No, I can't kill her. Actually it wasn't me who saved her – it was God. God saved her."

The Hutus began to flee, among them Vitale and his family. He explained to me that it was too dangerous to take me with them because I would be killed by other fleeing Hutus. However, staying put was also dangerous. Although most of the local Hutus had now left, the area was still full of retreating Hutu militiamen who were intent on killing anyone they encountered: both surviving Tutsis and any lingering Hutus, whom they would suspect of collaboration. Vitale told me to stay in the house until I was sure the area was in the hands of the Tutsis.

The next couple of days were terrifying. Our valley, with Vitale's house on one side and my family home on the other, lay right in the middle of the advancing Tutsis, who had reached as far as my old primary school, and the retreating Hutu army, who were held up near my grandfather's house. All night bombs and gun shots flew overhead, and I lived in fear that the house might be hit at any moment. Some food had been left in the house, which I cooked during the day. When there was a lull, I would run over to Vitale's brother's house next door to take food to my grandfather's brother, who had also been abandoned, coming back as quickly as I could.

After four days Vitale and his family returned. I think he must have reconsidered and decided that his best option was to use me as a safety valve. He took me outside and spoke to me privately. "Listen," he said, "you and I need to do business. I saved your life, now you're going to save me and my family. I'm not a bad man. I haven't killed anybody. You are going to talk to the Tutsis and tell them what I have done for you."

Soon after his return one of my father's Tutsi friends who had managed to survive, came to Vitale's house. He had heard I was there and wanted me to go with him to my old primary school, Gatagara, where all the Tutsi survivors were being taken for safety. "All the other orphans are there," he said. The mention of the word "orphan" provoked a very strong reaction in me. "I am not an orphan," I said. "I'm not going to go there until I find out if any members of my family are still alive. I don't want to go there." He left without me. I later discovered that all the Tutsis sheltering in the school had been kidnapped by Hutus and slaughtered.

Throughout the whole time I had been living with Vitale, there had also been a young man there. He was a twenty-year-old called Jacques and was related to Vitale on his mother's side, but his father was a Tutsi. Jacques had come to live with

Vitale at the start of the genocide, but since he was unknown in the area and all that people knew about him was that he was a relative, he was not in hiding and no one bothered him. Hearing that Nyanza was in Tutsi hands, he and I decided that we should try and make our way there. I said goodbye to Vitale and promised him that I would speak to the Tutsi leaders and tell them what he had done for me. I shall always be grateful to Vitale for the love he showed me in protecting me.

The one-and-a-half-hour walk to Nyanza was terrifying. Not only was there the deafening sound of bombs exploding first on one side and then on the other and the danger from stray bullets, but all along the road there were cruelly disfigured corpses. Some had clearly lain there for weeks; others were more recent. The smell was terrible. The whole way we did not meet a single living person.

As soon as we arrived in Nyanza, Jacques left me. He wanted to join the Tutsi fighters and take his revenge on the Hutus for what they had done. As we parted, I urged him, when it was all over, to go back and look after Vitale's family.

When he had gone, I did not know what to do. I tried a few houses where I heard they were taking in children who were on their own. At each door on which I knocked, I received the same response: they were full and could not take anyone else. I felt very alone and very vulnerable. I was filthy dirty, having worn the same clothes for three months; my hair was so encrusted that it had turned yellow and was ridden with lice. I was also suffering from malaria and for some days had been vomiting blood. It all suddenly became too much. I sat down by the side of the road and began to cry. And having started I could not stop. As I sat there sobbing uncontrollably, the world carried on around me. It began to rain.

After I had been sitting there for some time, my tears still flowing, a young man came over to me and asked me what was wrong. At first I could not speak. I could not stop crying. Trying to comfort me he told me he could take me to a place where they would look after me. Through my sobs I told him that I had tried everywhere and they were all full up. He said he knew a man who he thought might be able to help me.

He took me with him to find him. When we found the man, whose name was Musoni, he asked me about myself. I told him who my father and my grandfather were and he said that he knew them. In fact, he told me that he and some of the Tutsi fighters had gone to my grandfather's house hoping to save us but they had arrived too late.

"Are you the only person who survived?" he asked.

"I'm not sure," I replied. "There's a chance that one of the others might also have survived, in the same way I did."

He wanted to take me to stay with a friend of his, who, I discovered, lived in one of the houses I had already tried. When I explained that she had already told me she had too many children to care for, he said that as his friend he was sure she would take me in, which she did. As soon as I got to her house, I went straight to bed, without eating or having a bath. I was just too exhausted to do anything else.

The next three weeks passed in a blur. At first I was very sick, but as I recovered from the malaria, the full effects of the trauma set in. I kept myself to myself and avoided speaking whenever possible – I definitely couldn't cope with the endless teenage chatter of the other girls about their boyfriends. The woman who had taken me in, although very kind, had her hands more than full trying to care for so many in such difficult circumstances.

In the months that followed I gradually began to discover, one by one, which of the members of my wider family had survived. First of all, I discovered that one of the girls living in the same house was the daughter of my father's cousin. Her name was Venérand. Her brother, who had been studying in Belgium when the genocide started, had been searching for his family through the Red Cross. They found his mother first in a place called Ruhango, and she directed them to the Nyanza area where some of her children had been when the genocide started. When the Red Cross arrived to take her to her mother and her two surviving sisters, the girl refused to go without me. So I went with her to join her mother, who was living at the home of a Catholic priest, and we all stayed there. It meant so much to me to discover that some of my family had survived. I had thought I would never see any member of my family again. Later we were tracked down by another cousin, Clarisse, who was equally delighted to know that she was not alone.

After a few weeks of living with the Catholic priest, my father's cousin met a man she knew who was a major in the RPF. He took us all to live in a place called Byumba on the Ugandan border where he had a large property consisting of several houses. We lived in one of the houses and in another house were billeted some of his soldiers. In the aftermath of the genocide, when there was so much confusion, desolation and despair and no one was sure if they would find any members of their family left alive, people would open up their homes to anyone in need. It was a relief to be away from the main areas where the fighting had taken place. There was still some shooting going on and in many places there was the danger of unexploded bombs.

One day I was very frightened when a man in a soldier's uniform came to the house asking for me. I didn't recognize him, and the Major had instilled in us all to be very wary of strangers even if they claimed to be a relative, because it was not uncommon for children to be kidnapped by Hutus and murdered. I couldn't understand why anyone should come looking for me. I said to the man, "I'm not even going to talk to you because I don't recognize you." The man burst out laughing. Hearing his voice, I suddenly recognized that it was my Uncle Narcisse, the elder of my mother's two brothers who had joined the RPF, and I just jumped up into his arms and started crying. I tried to tell him that everyone else was dead, but he just said, "Shh, Frida. We'll talk later." He could not stay long as his battalion was passing through the area. Before he left, he told me that his brother was also searching for me.

My mother's other brother came to see me some months later. By this time my father's cousin and her family had been rehoused, but I was still living with the Major. Aware that I was extremely traumatized he wanted me to remain in the very secure environment of his home. On this occasion, too, I greeted my visitor very warily. My father's cousin had brought him to the house and they both stood knocking at the door.

"Who is it?" I asked through the door.

"Open the door and see," came the voice.

"I never open the door to strangers," I replied. "If you do not say your name, I won't open the door."

"Even if I say my name, you won't recognize me," he said. "Just open the door and see." I could hear the emotion in his voice.

I went to call one of the soldiers so that he could open the door. I looked at the man standing there, but I didn't recognize him.

"I am Mama's brother," he said.

"No, you're not," I said. "One of Mama's brothers is in the army and the other one is in Burundi, but neither of them has a beard."

The man pulled out a photograph and showed it to me. It was exactly the same photo that my mother had had of one of her brothers – without the beard. It was another emotional reunion!

Uncle Emile had come to take me back with him to Burundi. From there he was planning to send me to my mother's cousin in Gabon, who was willing to adopt me. The Major was away fighting at the time, and I was very reluctant to leave without asking his permission, but my uncle said that we would come back at a later date and speak to him. Before we left for Burundi, my uncle took me to say goodbye both to my father's cousin and her family and to the woman in Nyanza who had taken care of me in the first weeks after the genocide.

To my utter dismay, when we arrived in Burundi, a war had broken out there. I immediately regretted having decided to come back with my uncle. "You have brought me here to die," I said to him. My stay in Burundi was awful. I felt constantly afraid. I could not sleep and, when I did, I had the most terrible nightmares and I would have to go and sleep in my uncle's bed. In the nightmares I was always running, running, running … trying to get away. It was so terrifying that I was afraid to fall asleep. I could not bring myself to tell my uncle any of the details about what had happened – I was not yet ready to talk about it. I stayed with my uncle for three months until he had managed to sort out all the papers which I needed in order to travel to Gabon.

There was no direct flight to Gabon, so I had to change planes twice. I felt very anxious. For one thing, I had hardly ever seen a plane before, let alone fly on one and, of course, I was already feeling extremely vulnerable. My uncle's girlfriend worked at the airport and she asked one of my fellow passengers who was also Rwandan if he would keep an eye on me. She was not to know that this man was himself a Hutu killer fleeing justice in Rwanda. During the flight the man quizzed me about what was going on in Rwanda. He particularly wanted to know whether the situation was now reversed and the Tutsis were killing the Hutus. He also asked me penetrating questions about my family circumstances. I felt very uncomfortable talking to him and said as little as I could. Not wanting him to know that all my family had been killed and I was now on my own, I told him I was on my way to join my family in Gabon.

The first stop was at Dualla in the Cameroun. My uncle had arranged for someone he knew there to look after me until the flight to Gabon was due, but unfortunately this person simply failed to turn up. The Hutu man who was looking after me deposited me in a chair in the airport lounge and went off, purportedly to sort out some papers, but he simply never came back. So I was left waiting and waiting. When I eventually realized he wasn't going to come back, I didn't know what to do. I tried to speak to one of the airport staff, but I couldn't speak French and no one could speak Kinyarwanda.

In the end a policeman managed to find another passenger with the same passport as me, who was able to interpret. They nearly put me on a plane to the Ivory Coast, but just in time I realized that it was the wrong plane, and I kept repeating, "No, no, no...," until they looked at my ticket again and worked out that I was meant to be flying to Gabon. As the flight did not depart until 6.00 the next evening, I spent a whole night and a whole day waiting in the airport. Once at Libreville in Gabon, I had to take another flight to my final destination at Franceville, but since the connecting plane did not leave for two days, I stayed with a friend of the couple who were adopting me. I just slept solidly for the whole of those two days.

Although I was very grateful to my mother's cousin, Bernard Rutabana, and his wife, Gorette Baguma, for adopting me and very appreciative of all they were doing for me, the year and a half I spent in Gabon was extremely tough for me. I felt so alone. There was no one there who could possibly have any understanding of what I had been through, no one I could talk to. As well as the personal trauma I had endured I was coping with deep grief. In addition I was suffering ongoing physical problems as a result of the injuries I had incurred, with the injury to my head causing frequent swelling and painful headaches. I started school about three weeks after arriving in Gabon and had to adapt to learning in a totally new language. But this was easy in comparison with coping with the intense isolation and trauma I felt inside. So many times I would come home from school and lock myself in my room for days and days, crying and crying. I could not sleep. When I did sleep, I would wake up screaming in terror. I felt completely bereft.

Chapter 8

JULIENNE

In 1995, having returned to Rwanda for a visit, I refused to go back to Gabon. It was just such a relief to meet up with my cousin Adeline and be able to talk with someone who had been through what I had been through. My uncle Emile, who by now had returned from Burundi and was living in Kigali, didn't try to force me to go back: he said there was no point, and anyway my adopted parents were themselves planning to return to Rwanda soon. The decision was made that I would go to boarding school, and I asked to be allowed to return to the one I had attended before the genocide, which another cousin, Karaba, was also attending.

Being back in Rwanda and at the boarding school of my choice did not make life any easier for me. The three girls I shared a room with, including my cousin, were really friendly. Two of them had survived the genocide, and had therefore shared many of the same experiences I had and had suffered greatly. But there was one way in which I felt they could not relate to my experience. They were not alone as I was alone. Both of the girls still had their mothers, and my cousin also had her brother and her sisters. I felt so alone. My heart ached with grief.

The intense pain and crippling loneliness were there all the time – during every waking moment, and I was hardly able to sleep. When I went to bed I would fall asleep, only to wake in the middle of the night screaming in terror from my nightmares and then lie awake, crying and crying until my pillow was soaked through with my tears. I constantly had a terrible headache, which meant my schoolwork was suffering, and I was frequently in a bad mood. I felt really, really bad. I did not feel able to talk to anyone about what I was feeling. I cut myself off and withdrew into myself.

And salt was continuously being rubbed into my raw wounds by the fact that on a day-to-day basis I was being forced to interact with Hutus. My teachers were Hutus. My fellow pupils were Hutus. It was as if the genocide had never happened. My thoughts raged and rampaged in my head. How can these Hutus who killed my parents and my brothers and sisters now be teaching me in class? How can I be calmly sitting alongside Hutus as my classmates? These questions tormented me.

To make matters worse some Hutus tried to distance themselves from what had happened by pretending they were Tutsis. One day I was totally and utterly incensed by a conversation one of my room-mates relayed to me. I was getting dressed in my bedroom at the time. One of the Hutu girls, she told me, had actually had the audacity to say that I was really a Hutu. She claimed I was pretending to be Tutsi because my family had been killed when the Tutsis had taken control of the country after the genocide. I was so angry that, without even bothering to finish dressing, I went and found the girl and slapped her across the face.

It had all become too much for me. My head injury flared up

Few family pictures survived the genocide. The ones that did are now precious reminders of Frida's family.

001: From the left: sister – Solange Umugwaneza (Mimi), Frida, younger brother – Régis Dominique Shumbusho, house Boy – Mbangukira Welaris, brother – Alestide Munyabugingo, eldest Brother – César Uwineza, cousin – Alain Munezero. Everyone in this picture, except Frida, was killed in the genocide.

002. Normal times. Frida's parents (right) together with friends, Beatà and Placide whose two young boys were killed with Frida's family.

003. Frida's parents wedding day.

004. Frida's youngest brother, Régis, aged two years old, with mother – both died in the genocide.

005. Frida's grandparents from her father's side. Both died in the genocide.

006. Precious picture: Frida at seven years of age. The photograph is referred to in chapter 1.

007. Frida at fourteen years of age, four months after the genocide, remarkably bearing a smile.

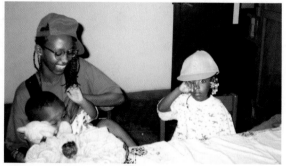

008. Frida's fifteenth birthday, with cousins Ken and Stella whose family adopted Frida.

009. Frida with her friends from boarding school. From the left: Ruth, Julienne (brought Frida to Christ), Toto Rachel, Frida and Toto Esther.

010. Frida (far left) at twenty years of age with some of the students that she led in her prayer group in APE Rugunga with Steven (on the right).

011. The remains of Frida's old home from the time of the genocide.

012. Frida standing in the trench where her family were killed.

013. The mass grave where Frida's family are now buried.

014. Mass grave of 1,900 bodies sited near her grandfather's house.

015. Sharing the story: Sandy Waldron, editor of the book, with Frida and son Maxwell at her old home.

016. A service in the Rwanda for Jesus Church where husband Steven is pastor.

017. Happy times: Frida and her pastor husband Steven with their two children, Natasha (2 yrs) and Maxwell (3 yrs).

018. Help in the UK – Tina & James Stacey.

019. A special cake celebrating the day Frida received Jesus as her personal Savior decorated with the words "God heals the broken-hearted."

again and I was sent to see a doctor at Kigali hospital for a check-up. As well as giving me some pills for the swelling, the doctor diagnosed that I had malaria and prescribed quinine. All the way back to school in the taxi I was planning how I would use these pills to commit suicide. I could not go on anymore.

When I got back to school one of my roommates, Huegette, found me crying in the toilet. "Why can't you talk to me, Frida?" she pleaded. "Just tell me what's bothering you."

I replied: "I can't tell you my problems – they're too heavy for you."

The next day I took an overdose. I took the tablets the doctor had given me to ease the swelling in my head, plus the malaria tablets and some aspirin. When my roommates found me, I was foaming at the mouth. "Frida is dying. Frida is dying," they screamed. I was taken to hospital where I remained in a coma for nearly three days.

When I regained consciousness, I was filled with utter despair. I felt so ashamed that I had not succeeded in my attempt to commit suicide. Anger burned within me – anger at the Hutus for destroying my family. I also felt totally insignificant and unloved. Without my family I felt I had lost my identity, my sense of belonging, my reason for living. Without those I loved and I knew had loved me I was nothing. There was no reason to go on living.

I couldn't bear people to know that I had tried to commit suicide – especially my relatives who would have been utterly shocked. So I made up a lie. I tried to make everyone believe that, having forgotten to take my malaria pills in the morning, I had doubled the dose at lunchtime. I don't suppose anyone was fooled.

✤ ✤ ✤

I went back to live with my adopted parents, who by now were also living in Kigali, and for a whole year I sat at home. With nothing else to occupy my thoughts, apart from my daily chores and playing with my adopted parents' two children, I brooded over my sense of isolation, my despair, my anger, my feelings of insignificance. The harrowing sleepless nights continued, wearing me down ever further. Night after night I would cry myself to sleep, only to wake up hours later screaming out, "They're going to kill me! I can see them ... I can see them ... They're going to kill me!" I was haunted by the images of what I had seen.

As a result of the suicide attempt, my adopted parents and wider family had now begun to realize the extent of the trauma I was suffering. It was arranged that I should attend the Trauma Center, which was a government initiative to help the deeply traumatized survivors of the genocide. It was woefully inadequate in the face of such overwhelming need. Out of all the people I saw at the Center, one young woman particularly stands out in my memory. Her name was Odette. She was only nineteen but she already looked old. She always covered her face with a scarf and she would never talk to anyone. I discovered that the lower part of her face and her shoulder had been obliterated by a gunshot wound. She later went to Europe for reconstruction surgery.

Each Tuesday and Thursday afternoon for two hours I would have an appointment with a psychiatrist and a woman who encouraged me to talk about my experiences, asking me such questions as, "How do you feel?" and "What are your dreams for the future?" On many occasions I didn't feel like talking and we all sat in silence.

At the Trauma Center we were each given a book and told to write down our thoughts and feelings in the form of a letter either to God or to someone you had lost. "Abuse God, if you want to," they said. "Tell Him how you feel. Express your feelings of anger towards Him." But for me it was a complete waste of time. You could write and write all you wanted – it did not make any difference. In the end I said, "This is rubbish. God is not listening to me. These people are not doing anything to help me." So I stopped going.

When the new school year began, I started to attend a local secondary school called APACOPE. By this time I was at least managing to get a bit more sleep. I joined the second year and my studies progressed well. I only had problems when my head injury flared up and terrible headaches stopped me doing my school work. I was in survival mode. But it didn't take much to make me angry, and my fellow students knew that it was best not to mess with me. I could not think about the future, but at least I was managing to make it through each day.

The following school year a new student joined our class. It was now 1998. Her name was Julienne Kabirigi. Like me she was eighteen and was a Tutsi. She had been born in Burundi and her family had not returned to Rwanda until after the genocide. It did not take long for the whole school to find out that Julienne was a born-again Christian and spent every spare moment she had telling her fellow students about Jesus Christ. At that time I hated believers. For me, all Christians were hypocrites and liars. I was frequently getting into heated arguments with the so-called Christians who tried to talk to me about God at school. In the genocide Christians had killed just like everyone else. I had no time for them and I had no time for God.

When Julienne first started at the school, she didn't know anyone. She would come to school on her own and go home on her own. She came across as a very quiet and serious person, but also quite self-contained. During the breaks she would sit on her own, with her Bible open in front of her, singing about Jesus in a loud, penetrating voice. If she wasn't singing, she would be reading her Bible, almost meditating, and often writing down notes. She came across as a very spiritual person. But whenever she got the chance, Julienne would start talking about Jesus. If she saw a group of students standing together and joking about, she would go over to them and start witnessing to them. Or if a teacher was late turning up to class, she would jump up and use the opportunity to start telling people what faith in God was all about. She really had no conversation apart from talking about God – which, of course, meant that most people avoided her like the plague and went very quiet when she was around.

"Just tell her not to come anywhere near me," I warned my friends. And they knew I was not joking. The previous year there had been another girl in our class who had always been talking about God and we had crossed swords more than once. I had thought she was a Hutu and when she talked about "repenting of my sins," I used to shout at her, "You go and repent yourself – with your family! I haven't got any sins." I would physically push her out of the classroom and on one occasion I threw her Bible out of the window.

I think Julienne must have got the message because she stayed clear of me. There was also an incident in class that must have confirmed to her that I could be quite a stroppy, awkward individual. It happened in an English class. Our English teacher, who was also a journalist and very strict – a very short man – had given the class a text to memorize and everyone was finding it very difficult. As one student struggled to recite the text, someone laughed in the general area of where I was sitting, in a group of six of us, including Julienne. The teacher was very angry. He thought it was me, but I said, "I didn't hear anyone laugh." (At that time I was form captain.) For some reason he completely overreacted and said that he was going to call the parents of the group of six into school, but first he wanted to see our behavior notebooks.

There was a points system in the school for behavior, which was recorded in these notebooks. Anyone going below twenty points landed themselves in serious trouble. He told us he was going to dock ten of our points and call all our parents into school. His talk of our parents made me really angry. I stood up and said, "How dare you talk about my parents! You don't know my parents. You have never met them!" I threw my notebook down in front of him and walked out of the classroom. All the other people in the class were amazed that I could talk like that to a teacher they all feared. I think Julienne was quite shocked too and realized that what she had been told about me was true.

So Julienne steered clear of me and I observed her from a distance. I could not help but be intrigued by her. There was something about her that I could not put my finger on. She seemed very different from the other Christians I had met. She was always singing. She was full of passion. I admired the way she was so bold about her faith, even standing up on buses and in the market-place in town to tell people about Jesus. But more than anything she seemed at peace. And that was the very thing I was desperate for. Peace. Something to help me make sense of my life. Something to help me understand why I had survived when all the rest of my family were dead.

As a little girl I had had a very strong faith in God. Each morning I had got up early to go to the six o'clock Mass before school and I had loved participating in the worship, either as a server or dancing in our traditional way. I had been deeply impressed and influenced by my grandfather's faith and godly lifestyle. Since the genocide, however, God had seemed a million miles away. I could not understand why He had abandoned my family when we needed Him most. I was confused and very angry.

For the next couple of months I continued to watch Julienne from a distance. Her life was impacting me without her even knowing it. One day I said to my friend Clare, "I am going to get Julienne to talk to me about Jesus, and I am going to become a believer."

"You become a believer?" she exploded. "If you become a believer, I will too!"

On another occasion I told my friend Karara that I wasn't interested in any more of his jokes because I was going to become a Christian. "If you become a believer," he teased, "then the whole school will get saved!" They had no idea that I was serious.

I felt I had to talk to Julienne. One morning, in the 10 o'clock break, I went up to her and asked her, "What is it that makes you sing all the time?"

"The peace of Jesus makes me sing," she answered.

"Can that same Jesus give me peace?" I asked.

Although she didn't know anything about me, she replied, "Oh yes, He can."

"Why don't you come and talk to me about Him, then? Why do you talk to other people, and never me?"

"I was planning to," she replied.

"When?" I pressed.

"Maybe later on today."

"Come and talk to me," I insisted. "I want to be a Christian."

Just then, one of my friends who had caught the tail-end of our conversation, interrupted, "She's lying. Don't believe a word of what she says. She hates Christians."

"Keep quiet," I snapped. "It's none of your business."

Later that morning Julienne came over to me and asked me to go with her to a lunchtime fellowship that she attended in the town. "No," I replied immediately. "There are so many killers in those fellowships. I don't want anything to do with them. I just want to become a Christian, find peace and get on with my life. Nothing else." She answered, "Well, there is no way you can grow as a Christian without being part of a fellowship."

Despite my blank refusal, the next day, which was 15 January 1998, before I went to school, I asked my adopted mum whether it was all right for me to go to the lunchtime fellowship with Julienne. "Yes," she said, "but just this once." So that lunchtime I went with her.

It was held in the Inkurunziza Church in Kigali, which was a two-mile walk from the school. I was amazed to see about a thousand people there. A man called Paul preached and I can remember thinking, "Julienne doesn't know anything about me. How can she have told this preacher all about me?" He preached about the suffering that the Rwandan people had endured, emphasizing that Jesus came to heal the broken-hearted. But out of everything that he said, what really struck me were the words: "Jesus can heal you . . . Jesus can heal you . . . Jesus can give you peace . . ."

When he called for people to come to the front, I rushed forward. He laid his hands on me and prayed for me. I was not alone. Thirty-five others were kneeling at the front with me.

It's hard to explain what happened to me that day, but I felt as though something had left me. I felt a huge sense of relief.

After everyone had been prayed for, we were all taken into a small room and Paul spoke to us. He explained that we were now born again and that our sins were forgiven.

We should now begin telling everyone about our new faith and should buy a Bible and start reading it. I thought to myself that I didn't have any money, but I would find some somehow.

I went outside and found Julienne, who was over the moon. We hugged each other and she said, "You're a believer now."

Chapter 9

A REASON TO LIVE AGAIN

From the time Jesus came into my life, I was a different person. I could sleep. I could sing. I could smile. I could begin to relate to people as friends, which I had found so difficult since the genocide. I was happy. Something in me had changed. I had found hope. I felt I could live again.

Within a few months of becoming a Christian the nightmares stopped and I no longer woke up in the night screaming out in terror. I found a Gideon New Testament I had been given at school and read it whenever I could – often when I should have been doing my schoolwork, which I now realize was not very wise. As I began to concentrate on God, I began to understand that there was a reason why I had survived the genocide. God's hand was upon my life and He had saved me for a purpose. I had thought that God had forgotten all about me. Now I began to realize that instead of my life being a big mess, it was a big miracle. My outlook was transformed.

However, from the start being a Christian was not easy. My family, although committed Catholics, in common with many in Rwanda at that time, were deeply suspicious of the new Pentecostal churches and fellowships that were having an impact in the country following the genocide. When after a very difficult period, they forbade me from attending the lunchtime fellowship at Inkurunziza, I felt I had to take a stand. Becoming a Christian had transformed my life. Time after time I tried to explain to my relatives the precious peace becoming a Christian had given me and the incredible sense of purpose that was growing within me, but they were not able to understand. Unwilling to jeopardize the progress I had now begun to make in my life, after a family conference at which I was given the ultimatum to choose between church and family, one morning I packed my possessions in one bag and left my adopted parents' home, having no idea where I could go. My uncle Gahaya who was a Catholic priest allowed me to live with him for a while but, without any financial support, life was very difficult. Being able to grow in my new-found faith had become a matter of life or death to me. I could not stop now.

It was during this difficult time that I started attending Julienne's church, which was called Rwanda for Jesus Church. I simply responded to a suggestion she made that I could come and see what it was like. The first time I went I did not see the pastor, Steven Gashumba, whom Julienne had told me so much about, as he was preaching at a church in Butare, a two-hour drive away. His brother Stanley was preaching that Sunday.[4] I sat at the back, so that I could watch what was going on. I liked the church. At one point in the service, people started talking in a different language but, knowing the pastor had grown up in Uganda, I thought they must be speaking in Luganda. I didn't realize that they were speaking in languages given to them by the Holy Spirit. The following Sunday I returned to Rwanda for Jesus Church and made the

---

4. Julienne is now married to Stanley!

decision to make it my church. Not long after I joined the worship team and threw myself into the life of the church.

After a couple of months I began to realize that, although God had provided me with a wonderful church family, I could not cope with the present situation much longer. Having no money to take the bus, the eight-mile walk to school and back each day was taking its toll and my studies were suffering. Occasionally Christians from Inkurunziza or church, knowing my circumstances, would give me money to catch the bus home, but most days I had to walk – and on an empty stomach too, as I had no money to buy lunch. The end of the school year was approaching and I decided that, even though it would be a wrench to leave Julienne and the church, it would be better if the following school year I went back to boarding school. But I was determined to find a school where I would be free to pray and worship and to speak openly about my faith.

My cousin Adeline was at a boarding school in Nyanza called ESPANYA, which stood for Ecole Sécondaire des Parents de Nyanza. She told me that there were a lot of believers at the school and encouraged me to join her there. When I went to the school with my cousin to ask if there was a place available in Senior 4, I was really surprised to find that the administrator of the school was Musoni, the man who had helped me at the end of the genocide and had found a home for me to stay in. He was very happy to give me a place at the school, and this seemed to confirm that it was the right step for me. Julienne was heartbroken when I told her about my decision. By this time we had developed a really close friendship and we both found it hard to say goodbye.

Term started a month later. There was just enough income

from renting out my father's house in Kigali to pay for the school fees and to buy my school uniform and equipment. As I started yet another school I had two specific goals in mind: the first to serve God with all my heart and, the second, to study hard and pass all my exams with good grades. By the end of my first week at the school, however, I was feeling rather depressed and deflated by the group of Christians I had met there. They insisted that you couldn't be a Christian if you wore trousers or ear-rings, and they said that women should cover their heads in church. The Christian faith I had embraced had brought me life and freedom. I could not understand their legalism, and I didn't want anything to do with it.

About the third week of term I was just coming out of the school shop, where I had bought an avocado to add to the awful-tasting beans and rice we were served for lunch every single day, when I saw someone I recognized entering the school. It was Julienne's brother Majege and he was carrying a huge bag. When I saw the person following in behind him, I just couldn't believe my eyes. It was Julienne! I ran up to her and gave her a big hug! I was so surprised and excited to see her. "What are you doing here?" I asked her. Julienne herself was rather dazed and confused. That morning when she had woken up, she had had no idea that she would be changing schools that day! On her way back from morning prayers at Rwanda for Jesus Church, her brothers had bundled her into a car and brought her to the school. Their aim was to stop Julienne's evangelistic activities, but nothing could stop her.

Julienne had never been to boarding school before so I helped her settle in and showed her the ropes. Since there were not enough beds at the school everyone had to share. I shared with my cousin Adeline. I was really glad that Julienne was able to share with a lovely fellow believer called Genie.

Julienne and I were both convinced that God had a reason for bringing us back together and was going to do something very exciting at the school.

The very first evening Julienne came to the school we were all in our huge dormitory just getting ready to go to bed when I heard someone trying to gain everyone's attention. That was quite common as there were often announcements that had to be made, so I turned to look. I will never forget what I saw. The person trying to attract everyone's attention was Julienne and she was standing on top of one of the bunk beds that filled the room. In true African style the enormous room was jam-packed with bunk-beds leaving only a tiny passageway between for the girls to squeeze through.

She shouted out, "I want to tell you all about Jesus who is willing to save anyone who will come to Him." She then proceeded to tell the 300 girls in the dormitory that they needed to receive Jesus as their Lord and Savior. At the end she asked everyone to close their eyes while she prayed. Although rather bemused, everyone respected her request. That evening six girls gave their lives to Christ and many others were interested. They just couldn't believe that some-one so new to the school could have the courage to do what she had just done. It was an unforgettable experience. By the time Julienne had been at the school a week, everyone knew her.

All the Christians in the school were encouraged by Julienne's bold stand and the Christian group had an influx of members. A couple of weeks later, two of the girls who went to Kigali Restoration Church when they were at home told us that the church was holding a forty-day fast, and we decided to join them "in the spirit." Each morning we woke up early and had a time of prayer at 3.00 a.m. – it was my job to creep around all the beds in the dark waking everyone up.

We then fasted until 6.00 p.m. each evening, also meeting to pray and read the Bible each lunchtime and evening. We broke our fast with a meal of rice mixed with black beans in water and had mild black tea without sugar. It did not taste very good, but it kept us going. Fasting was a radical new idea for the Church in Rwanda at that time and, to tell the truth, we didn't know much about it. We even thought it was wrong to swallow any water when we were washing our teeth! By the end of our fast we had seen miracles of people coming to Christ both inside and outside of the school.

Trouble was brewing, however. Some of the girls fell sick and the headmaster discovered that it was because they had been fasting. One girl had to be sent home because she became so ill, and her parents came to the school to complain. Julienne, as the leader of the group, was summoned to the headmaster's office and she was told that the fasting must stop. When she said that she was not prepared to stop it, she was suspended and sent home while the situation was dealt with. Before she left, Julienne told me to lead the group in her absence.

The following Sunday Julienne was due to preach at a local church in Nyanza, Eglise Prespétarienne au Rwanda, which was the church we used to attend each Sunday. When the pastor came to the school to talk to Julienne about it and discovered that she was not there, he asked to speak to me and invited me to preach instead. I told him that I had never preached before, but he seemed convinced I could do it and eventually I agreed. It was a huge challenge for me to stand up in front of a congregation of over a hundred people and the elders of the church and I was terrified.

Sitting at the front of the church alongside the pastor, I kept my eyes firmly shut until the time for me to preach came. As I stood up everyone cheered and clapped their hands. Sweating and shaking with fear I preached for the next forty-five minutes, speaking about what had happened to me and about God's power to change lives. At the end I asked people to come forward if they wanted to give their life to Jesus, and nearly the whole congregation came and knelt at the front, crying out to God and repenting of their sins. It was amazing. It showed me what God can do, when we trust in Him and not in ourselves. From that day I began to feel a call on my life to preach.

After a few days Julienne returned to the school accompanied by her sister. When the headmaster explained the problems Julienne had been causing, her sister confessed that the reason the family had sent her to boarding school was because they could not control her and because she was causing similar problems at her previous school with her preaching activities. Warning Julienne that if she was expelled, her parents would not pay school fees for her at another school, she begged the headmaster to give her sister another chance. Julienne insisted that she could not stop herself talking about Jesus, because it was her life.

Stipulating that the younger girls must stop fasting, the headmaster eventually agreed that the students would be allowed to pray at certain allotted times – but not very early in the morning! Julienne was accepted back into the school. I think that, in fact, the headmaster had noticed that the fasting had had a positive impact on the school and seen that the behavior of many of the most difficult pupils had improved. Even in the town, people were talking about how the school had changed.

Knowing that we had to curb our activities within the school, Julienne came up with a new plan. Each Sunday, which was our only free day, she would take us out into the town to preach in the market-place after church. One person would preach and then the rest of us would talk to anyone who was interested. As a group of girls working together we were often the butt of jokes and a great deal of teasing from the lads who worked on the stalls, but it was worth it to see people coming to Jesus. Later on, we started going to the hospital, where we would do washing for the patients, many of whom had been abandoned by their families. Working alongside Julienne, I began to grow in confidence. I had caught her passion to spread the gospel and I never wanted to lose it.

Chapter 10

TOO EVIL TO FORGIVE

I was growing as a Christian and passionate about God, but there was one topic I did not like to hear preachers talk about. I used to shut my ears whenever it came up. It was the topic of forgiveness. Sometimes preachers from Uganda and the West, knowing what the Rwandan people had been through, would come to the lunchtime fellowship and speak very strongly about the need for us to forgive. But I used to say to myself, "These people can only talk about forgiveness because they have no idea of what we have been through."

The examples the preachers used to give of situations in which they found themselves required to forgive seemed so trivial – even laughable – compared to what had happened to me. An argument with their wife, a misunderstanding between friends, a broken promise, even the betrayal of infidelity in marriage: all these paled into insignificance when I considered what I had to forgive. What right did they have to lecture me on the subject? So I closed my ears to the preachers who spoke on forgiveness and my eyes to the Bible verses which challenged me. No way, God, no way! I had every reason not to forgive.

While nothing could take away the peace and joy I had found when I had met Jesus on that day back in January, my day-to-day life was hard. The loss of my family had left a gaping hole, the pain of which I felt every day. There was no one who really cared whether I lived or died; no one to share with me the ups and downs of daily living. I was an orphan. Totally alone in the world. Nothing was ever going to change that. Nobody could ever give me back what I had lost.

And if the constant daily ache in my own heart was not enough, I was living in a country which was still reeling from the catastrophic events that had taken place. I was surrounded, on the one hand, by deeply traumatized people who could barely make it through to the end of each day and, on the other hand, by people who were doing their best to pretend that the genocide had never happened or at least that they had had no part in it. People were living side by side with the killers who had destroyed their lives. To all intents and purposes they were getting away with it.

The sense of purpose and destiny that God had given me for my life was providing me with the strength to go forward. I was focused and determined. Whenever the disturbing topic of forgiveness came up, I would say, "God, I will do whatever You want me to do. I will go and preach the gospel in the villages. I will fast. I am prepared to be persecuted for Your name's sake. I will do anything. But I will never forgive the people who destroyed my family."

Forgiveness was, however, a subject that would not go away. Every time I went to church I was worshiping alongside Hutus and I could not stop the anger and bitterness I felt in my heart from rising. It seemed that so often when I sat down and read the Bible, a verse about forgiveness would spring off the page or when I heard a sermon it was the words "You need to forgive" that sounded louder than all the others. The challenge of forgiveness came to me over and over again.

Everything within me screamed out at the very idea of what God was asking me to do. It made me feel almost physically sick. It was not to be countenanced, not even to be entertained. What those men had done to my family and to me was too evil to forgive. I could never forgive them for murdering my family in front of my eyes. If it had not been for God's miraculous intervention I would be dead too. They had ripped my life apart and savagely destroyed everything.

And if that evil were not terrible enough, I knew that others had suffered just as much horror and some even worse. I had heard of people herded into churches and massacred. I had heard of pregnant women who, moments after giving birth, had watched their innocent new-born babies being slaughtered and then been brutally raped by the murderer. I had heard of men deliberately infecting women with AIDs. I had heard of young women gang-raped until they dropped down dead; of tiny, innocent babies being thrown against walls to kill them ... No, these horrors were too great. They could never be forgiven. These killers must be punished. They must be made to pay for what they had done.

Whenever the subject of forgiveness came up, I would be thrown into turmoil and angry and bitter thoughts would crowd into my mind. But, despite my stubborn refusal to listen, nothing would make God's quiet but insistent voice go away. My argument with God would run along these lines: "Lord, why do You keep talking to me about forgiveness when I am not ready to forgive? How can I even begin to forgive people for what they have done? I wouldn't know where to start. Yes, I can forgive the girl at school for telling lies about my family. Yes, I can forgive somebody who has insulted me. Yes, I can forgive a family member for beating me unfairly. Yes, I can forgive those who laugh at me for being a Christian. But how can I ever forgive those brutal murderers who destroyed everything I love – my parents, my brothers and sisters, my grandparents, my home. Who never showed any mercy but wanted to wipe my tribe off the face of the earth? Who have taken everything I have so I am left with nothing? How, Lord? No, You are asking too much. I can't go to these people and tell them I forgive them for what they have done."

But God would not give up. Again and again He placed the challenge of forgiveness before me. "Will you forgive as I forgive?" "No, God," I persisted. "You cannot ask this of me. Haven't I been through enough? You can send me to the farthest corner of the globe and I will willingly go, but You cannot ask me to forgive the Hutus who destroyed my life and everything I loved."

The debate within me raged on over months and God did not let it drop. I read Jesus' parable about a king who wrote off the huge debts of one of his servants but was extremely angry when the forgiven man would not show the same mercy to a fellow servant, who by comparison owed him a very small sum. In the story the king turned the man over to the jailers to be imprisoned and tortured until he paid back all he owed, saying in conclusion, "This is how my heavenly Father will treat each of you unless you forgive your brother from your heart" (Matthew 18:35). I tried to reason that He couldn't possibly be speaking about such enormous crimes as murder and genocide. Surely God made allowances for people like me who had suffered such great loss?

As I went back to this passage again and again, trying to come to terms with the huge challenge it presented, God began to show me that lying masked behind the immense sense of injustice that I felt was another much less noble emotion: self-pity. I wanted the world to look at me and say, "Poor Frida. Look what she has suffered." I was cradling my loss to myself and using it as my comfort blanket. I wanted people to feel sorry for me, but God showed me that no child of His ever needed to be pitied. I began to understand that self-pity was a monster that would devour me if I continued to give in to it.

Once I was willing to face up to the self-pity in my heart, to ask God for His forgiveness and allow the Holy Spirit to change my attitude I was able to move on in my thinking about forgiveness. From a blank refusal even to contemplate making such a step, I began to consider what the consequences might be if I refused to obey God. Just suppose I refused to forgive the killers of my family. What would be the result in my own life and how would it affect my service of God? God, I knew, would never allow me to be a preacher of His love if unforgiveness remained in my heart. Refusing to forgive would staunch the flow of God's love in my own life. Bitterness and resentment would take over and work like a cancer to destroy me. I imagined myself becoming old well before my years and people pointing the finger as I went about my life, saying, "She's the one who survived the genocide, but her life finished when she refused to forgive those who wiped out her family."

One thing I was sure about was that God had not saved my life from the grave so that I could struggle on through the rest of my life, withered up inside. He wanted to use me as someone through whom His love could flow and be an inspiration to others to get hold of His love. Yet still, as I argued back and forth, the mountain that God was placing before me, seemed too immense, too arduous, insurmountable.

I did not speak to anyone about the challenge I was being given by God. I prayed about it continually and I also spent days fasting, asking God to help me to do what He was asking me to do. So desperate was I to find breakthrough in this area of my life that each Friday I prayed through the night, pleading with God to guide me and help me.

Time and time again as I wrestled with the subject of forgiveness, I came back to two key passages in the Bible. The first was Luke 23:34 where, as Jesus is dying on the cross, He cries out, "Father, forgive them, for they do not know what they are doing." I began to realize that, like my family, Jesus had been hounded and hated to the point where He had been murdered by members of His own people. He had been persecuted as we had been persecuted. He had been tortured and abused as we had been. And, in the end, He had been murdered as my family had been. There was great comfort for me in knowing that God's own Son had suffered in the way that I had suffered, but for a long time I could not get any further. "Yes," I reasoned, "but Jesus was God. As God He could forgive His murderers, but I am a human being and not God."

It was many months of agonizing before the breakthrough came and I understood for the very first time that, yes, the Jesus who was nailed to the cross was 100 percent God, but He was also 100 percent man. When the nails were driven through His hands and He was hung on a cross, He had a human body just like me, He felt the pain as I did, and yet He could still say, "Father, forgive them . . . "

The second key passage was Acts 7, which records how one of the first believers, Stephen, was stoned to death for his faith in Jesus – the first Christian martyr. Like Jesus, in the midst of his suffering and pain, Stephen was able to forgive those who were killing him. As he lay dying, he cried out, "Lord, do not hold this sin against them." Stephen was a human being just like me. He had no greater resources than I had to enable him to forgive his murderers. God the Holy Spirit had enabled him to forgive. I understood that if Stephen could forgive, then I could too. As I allowed this insight to change my thinking and soften my heart, I began to put myself in the place of Stephen and imagine myself saying, "Lord, do not hold this sin against them," as he did when the stones were being hurled against his body.

As the Holy Spirit revealed more and more to me, I began to understand that at the time of the genocide the devil had taken over my country and there was a spirit behind the people who had perpetrated these terrible crimes. It was the devil who had driven the Hutus to fulfill their stated aim of exterminating every single Tutsi. There was no other way to explain the speed in which the bloodlust had swept through the country, or the depths of depravity to which the killers had sunk. They had torn babies out of the womb, they had put tiny babies inside cooking pots and smashed them to death. They had committed unspeakable crimes of brutality against women; they had buried people alive ... These killers had decorated their bodies with their victims' limbs and had drunk human blood!

Although many of the killers were high on drink and drugs, I knew that something must have overtaken them to sink to those levels of depravity. Even Hutus living in the most remote areas of the country, who had no access to the radio stations pumping out their poisonous message of hate and destruction, had joined in perpetrating these atrocious acts. The only explanation could be that an utterly evil power had compelled them. As Jesus had died on the cross, He had cried out, "Father, forgive them, for *they do not know* what they are doing," and I began to understand that the Hutus, too, had not known what they were doing. Although this in no way absolved them from their individual and collective responsibilities for their crimes,

I knew they were swept up into something that was beyond their control.

I also considered the shameful truth that many who claimed to be Christians had participated and even taken the lead in the killings – even reading from the Bible to justify the acts they were about to commit. I then realized that it is not those who say they are Christians who are Jesus' true followers but those who do what He commands. Jesus was asking me to forgive my enemies. If I wanted to be His disciple there could be no doubt about what I should do. I began to realize that I could not go on being part of the worship group at church and taking part in other church activities if I was not willing to forgive. I would be a hypocrite – the very thing in my mind I was often accusing Hutu Christians of being.

Very gradually, over a period of months, God brought me to the point where I was able to say, "Lord, I *want* to forgive." This was a momentous step forward, but I still felt over-whelmed by the sense that it was totally beyond my capacity to do so. I did not have the resources inside me; I did not know where to begin. My cry was, "Lord, I want to be like You. I want to put my feet into Your footprints. I want to obey You, but I can't in my own strength. In my strength, I can't forgive the people who have destroyed my life. But I know I am Your child, and I ask You to give me a new heart and the courage to follow Your example."

Two months later I felt the Lord God had answered my prayer. Perhaps the final stepping stone in this long and harrowing process had been the realization that both Jesus and His disciple Stephen had not waited for their enemies to come to them to ask for forgiveness, but had taken the initiative in forgiving those who were about to take their lives away from them. I realized that God was asking me to take the first step by going and telling my family's murderers that I forgave them. I needed to step out in faith, believing that He would do the rest.

I decided to begin with the man who had killed my father. I asked my cousin Emmanuel, who was not a believer, to go with me to the prison in a village near our family home, where I knew he and some of the other local men who had killed people in the genocide were being held.

"I've heard that you have become a Christian," Emmanuel said. "What are you planning to do at the prison?"

"I just want to see the killers, that's all." I was deliberately vague.

When we arrived at the prison, we asked one of the warders on duty whether we would be allowed to see François, my father's killer. He said we could, but explained that he was on a labor gang building some new houses a short distance away from the prison and would need to be fetched – it wouldn't take long. As we stood waiting, I caught sight of some of my former neighbors among the prison inmates and was suddenly gripped with an awful fear. "What am I doing here?" I asked myself. "Am I doing the right thing? What am I going to say to him?" As the prison warder returned bringing François, the fear intensified and I felt absolutely terrified. "What if he has got some kind of weapon in his pocket?" I whispered to my cousin.

"Don't be afraid," he reassured me. "He is powerless now."

François stood in front of me, arms folded and leaning back on one foot, a dismissive sneer spread right across his face, as if to say, "What do you want?" I wanted to reach out and shake his hand, but I was suddenly overwhelmed by uncontrollable emotion. I burst into tears and dropped down on the ground, curling myself up into a little ball with my arms covering my head.

"What's happening to you? What's happening to you?" my cousin asked.

"Take me home," I sobbed. I needed to get out of there.

I was not ready. The sight of the man who in cold blood had murdered my father had opened the floodgate of all the raw emotions which were still locked up so tightly inside me. I had thought I was ready, but when the moment came I could not go through with it. I cried all the way home in the bus. Later that night and in the days that followed, I wept before God and cried out, "God, why are You torturing me like this? Can't You see now that I can't do it? You know I want to, but I can't. I will only be able to do it if You give me Your heart."

A year later, and after much more prayer, I felt ready to make a second attempt to forgive. First of all, I went to try and see John, the man who had nearly killed me. When I discovered that he had been killed by a bomb while fleeing to the Congo, I went to visit his sister and told her that I had come to her, in John's place, to tell her that I had forgiven him and had released him from what he had done. On hearing my words, she cried.

Then I went back to the neighborhood in which I had grown up and went from door to door telling everyone that I had found Jesus and I wanted to let them know that I had forgiven them. On hearing my words, several people gave their lives to Jesus.

Perhaps the most poignant encounter was with an old neighbor called Elina, whose daughter had occasionally come to do her family's washing at the standpipe with me. The family were Seventh Day Adventists. Like John, Elina's husband Jason had also been killed while fleeing to the Congo. As I sat in her home and explained why I had come, I could see cupboards taken from our home filled with our old plates and cups and glasses and she and her children were wearing our old clothes. Thirsty from speaking, I asked her for a glass of water and, as she brought it to me, there was a flash of recognition that she was about to hand me my own glass and she hesitated, very embarrassed. I quickly said, "I have not come to take anything from you. I have come to make peace with you." I drank the water and prayed for her family. My neighbor herself just shook her head and opened her mouth as if to speak, but she could not find any words. Shortly afterwards I left her home with the words, "Peace be with you."

As I made my way home on the bus, this time I was rejoicing. I was so grateful to God that He had given me the courage to do what I had done and that some people had even turned to Him. At the same time, however, I was very aware of how these people were suffering. In their eyes I could see their fear that I had come to take my revenge and I could also see very clearly that they were not at peace. Not only that, but they were struggling to make ends meet and were becoming poorer and poorer. Where previously they had worked for people like my father, the employment situation now was very difficult and many people had no work. This understanding fuelled my prayers and now I was truly able to say from my heart, "Father, forgive them for they did not know what they were doing."

In time I was able to return to the prison and on this second occasion I was able to deliver my message of forgiveness. I sat down with François, the man who had killed my father, and he told me the whole story of what had happened.[5] It seems that when they had finished with my family, Papa could stand it no longer. He came down from his hiding place and gave

---

5. Although he later denied it (see chapter 14).

himself up to them. He was forced to dig his own grave and told to wait by it while the killers went off to have their lunch. When they returned, they found him waiting – I believe that, having seen his whole family murdered, death had over-whelmed him. He asked for time to pray before they killed him and François told me that as my father said "Amen," he killed him. An eyewitness has since told me that my father was forced to remove the dungarees and socks he was wearing before he was killed, which were taken by François, and was therefore murdered and buried naked.

I asked him to tell me where my father's grave was but he said he could not remember. When I pressed him, he told me a place but when we dug there, we could not find anything. Not long afterwards François and many like him were released from prison. If people confess what they have done, they are set free.

I had set out on the process of forgiveness because I understood that this was what Jesus was asking me to do. What I discovered was that, as I did so, forgiveness brought me great healing within myself. On becoming a Christian, I had found a new peace, but this peace increased immeasur-ably as I forgave the people who had destroyed my life.

I once met a Hutu man who had become a Christian in prison, after having been sentenced for his part in the atrocities. As we talked together, I asked him what had pushed him as a Hutu to do what he had done. He told me that they had acted under pressure from the government.

"What if the Hutus were in the same position again?" I asked. "Would you do the same thing again?"

"No," he answered. "Having seen what I have seen, I could never do the same thing again."

Our conversation moved on to the subject of forgiveness. I asked him if he had ever gone to the families of those he had killed to ask for their forgiveness. He replied that he had confessed his sins to God, and that was enough: he did not need to ask for forgiveness from anyone else. Taking his hands in mine I said, "You should go and ask for forgiveness from the people you have harmed and make peace with them. Otherwise blood will always be on your hands. There are so many people who are still crying because of what they have suffered at your hand. You need to go to them and ask them to forgive you."

"No," he said, "God has forgiven me, and that is enough. I know you will never forgive me."

"I have forgiven you," I said.

As I set out on the pathway of forgiveness and saw first hand the great pain that was in my nation as a result of the genocide, God began to give me a vision to help the broken-hearted people of Rwanda to find healing. I had the idea that, instead of celebrating my twentieth birthday on 14 March (the day I was born), I would celebrate it on 15 January, the day I had become a Christian two years before and I would tell my friends about the vision God was giving me to help those who were still in deep pain. On my birthday cake were written the words "God heals the broken-hearted." When the time came to eat the cake, I made a short speech to my friends, including my pastor Steven.

"The reason that the words 'God heals the broken-hearted' are on this cake and not 'Happy Birthday' is because today I am celebrating the fact that God has healed my heart. God has given me a vision to help other people and I know that one day the Lord will make a way for me to have full knowledge of how to help the hurting and traumatized people, and the orphans and other people who have gone through so much.

When I was born, my parents gave me the name Umuhoza, which means 'counselor' or 'comforter.' I believe that, although they did not know it at the time, it was a prophetic name. I want to do what this name means: I want God to give me a heart to comfort people who are really suffering and show them that God can heal their broken hearts."

Chapter 11

SURPRISED BY LOVE

For a while before my twentieth birthday celebration my pastor Steven had begun to play an increasingly important role in my life. Steven was, and still is, very highly respected as the pastor of Rwanda for Jesus Church, which he had founded four years before in 1996. He is an excellent preacher and I really enjoyed being a part of his church. Nine years my senior, I viewed him as older and wiser. I suppose I was in awe of him. As well as at church, I often used to bump into him at the lunchtime fellowship which he also used to attend sometimes.

There was, however, one thing that really annoyed me about him – he could never seem to remember my name. We had been introduced several times but by the next time we met he had always forgotten my name again. I thought to myself, "What kind of a pastor is this who can't even remember my name!" Still, he was a busy man, I reasoned to myself, and he was meeting people all the time.

At our church there was a service every evening and I would always attend. I would arrive early and sit quietly at the back waiting for it to begin; I tended to keep myself to myself. One evening my friend Sonia came over to talk to me and I was really surprised by what she had to say. She told me that the pastor had three young people whom he had "adopted" as his spiritual children – she was one of them – and now he wanted to make me a fourth. I was stunned because I couldn't believe he was even aware of who I was but I was happy to agree. I found out later that Steven had asked Sonia to talk to me about this several times previously but for some reason she had never done so.

Not long afterwards I was waiting at the bus stop on my way to church when Steven joined the queue and we started chatting. He began to probe a little into my background.

"Do you live with your mum and dad?" he inquired.

"No, I don't live with any of my family," I replied.

"Who gives you the money you need to get around?" he wondered.

"God gives me the money," I said.

"Have you got any brothers or sisters?"

"No," I answered. "I haven't got any brothers or sisters."

"What happened to them?" he persisted.

"They were all killed in the genocide."

My admission stunned him and, more gently now, he began to probe further into my past. When he had discovered the extent of my loss in the genocide, he said with amazement in his voice, "I would never have thought you were a survivor of the genocide. The way you conduct yourself I thought you were from Burundi, not Rwanda, and that you were the daughter of a rich family ... I thought you were from outside, not from this country ... The trouble you've suffered does not show on your face."

I didn't know how to reply and, after a few minutes of awkward silence, the conversation changed direction. When the bus didn't come, he decided to take a taxi to the church, and I climbed in with him. Just before we arrived at the church, he asked me whether I would meet up with him after church on Sunday and tell him the whole story of what I went through in the genocide. I said I would. The following Sunday, after I had shared my whole story with him, he sat silently for a while, clearly shocked by what he had heard, and then he said, "I'm very sorry that for so long I failed to realize that I had somebody in my congregation who had been through what you've been through. Please forgive me for not having taken notice of you and especially that I kept forgetting your name. I'm really sorry!"

Steven asked me to take him back to my village and show him where everything had happened, which I did soon afterwards. I explained to him about the journey of forgiveness that God was taking me on and pointed out to him the various Hutu neighbors I had visited and tried to be reconciled with. He took a deep interest in it and gradually we became very good friends.

As our friendship developed I realized that Steven was beginning to see me in a different way. It was no longer the relationship of a spiritual father to a child, but a much more equal relationship. There was even a little thought at the back of my mind that he was beginning to see me as a woman. But whenever this thought popped into my head, I immediately quashed it and told myself that it was the devil putting it there. A pastor didn't look at the members of his congregation in that way!

This was where our relationship stood at my twentieth birthday party, at which I had asked Steven to pray for me. He encouraged me to take hold of the vision God had given me for my life and see it come into being. In the weeks and months that followed, our friendship strengthened, and Steven would often come to me and ask for my advice about some of the church issues he was facing. I couldn't believe the trust he was placing in me. No one had ever done that before! No one had ever talked to me on an adult-to-adult level and actually listened to what I had to say – even acted on what I had to say. It made a deep impact on me.

Sometimes when Steven was invited to preach at other churches, he would take me with him and give me a twenty-minute slot to share my testimony. One day, on the way home from one of these preaching engagements, he turned to me and said, "Would you mind being my spiritual sister instead of my daughter?" I laughed and said, "Of course not," but in my head I was asking myself, "What kind of a pastor is this?"

I was now in my fifth year of secondary education and very focused on making up for lost time. My aim was to finish my schooling and then serve God for the rest of my life. In the course of our long talks Steven would occasionally ask my advice about what to do about some of the young women who were showing rather too much interest in him. Without hesitation I would tell him that the call of God was on his life and he should never rush into anything as life-changing as marriage. "Just break it off," I would say, rather ruthlessly. I too had my fair share of admirers, but I never paid them a moment's attention.

One evening we went out to our favorite restaurant. I remember it was a Tuesday evening and Steven was due to go to Kenya for a conference the following day. I felt rather keyed up. There was something about the way that Steven had spoken about the evening that was bothering me. I got the impression that there was something he wanted to say. As we ate our meal we chatted normally, but over a cup of tea Steven began to tell me a little parable-like story. "What would you do," he asked rather coyly, "if you were renting a small house and, in the foundations of that house, you discovered there were some bars of gold, and you were the only one who knew they were there?"

Quick as a flash I replied, "I would do my best to buy the house and then, as soon as it was mine, I would knock it down and dig out the gold. Then I would sell the gold and develop a business, so that I could build my own house."

"Oh," he said. A couple of moments later he asked, "What would you do if you were a musician surrounded by many excellent players and you discovered that your own child had an even more amazing musical gift than they did?"

"I would train the child," I said immediately, "and do everything within my powers to ensure that he or she got the chance to become the best musician he or she could possibly be."

By now I was shaking, beginning to suspect he was about to say something that I did not want to hear at all.

"Frida," he continued, "we've known each other quite a long time now, and I have discovered that you are that small house and you are that child."

I couldn't believe what I was hearing.

"I asked you first to be my spiritual child, then I asked you to be my sister: now I want to ask you to be my wife."

By now I was shaking so much that he asked me, "Are you afraid?"

"No, no, I'm not," I stuttered.

Steven went on: "I don't want you to accept me because I am your pastor; I want you to accept me because you love me and you have prayed about it and know that it is God's will."

I didn't give his proposal a minute's thought. "No, no, I'm very sorry, but I'm not ready to get married. I haven't even thought about getting married. Please forget you ever asked me."

"Please don't say no without thinking about it," he asked. "Go home and think about it and pray about it. For the sake of our friendship, please think about it."

"No," I said, very firmly. "I don't want to pray about it. I know the answer right now. I'm not going to waste any time thinking and praying about it."

"Even if you know your answer, please don't tell me yet," he persisted. "Tell me your answer when I get back from Kenya."

While Steven was away, if, as I sat on the school bus, I remembered that he had proposed to me, I would shake my head and think, "No way. God, I'm very sorry. I know he's a man of God and he's your servant, and I respect him as my pastor, but there is no way I could ever marry him." One of my main objections was that he seemed so much older than me. True to my word, I did not pray about it at all while he was away.

The day Steven was due to get back, I was at school leading our large Christian fellowship when he walked in, carrying his briefcase. Arriving back from Kenya, instead of going home he had come straight to the school. I was standing at the front giving a talk and my heart sank when he walked in. When I had finished, although I really didn't want to, I greeted him publicly and gave him an opportunity to speak to my fellow students – he was my pastor after all. After the meeting had finished, he asked me whether we could meet that evening after the church service. I told him I was in the middle of exams and had so much work to do that I wouldn't even be able to attend the service. Later I relented and went down to give him my answer. I told him very firmly that I had no intention of getting married until I was at least twenty-six; God had given me a vision for my life and I intended to run with it. "OK," he said, "let's just leave it at that then."

In the months that followed Steven asked me two more times to marry him, but my answer remained the same. He never exerted any force or pressure on me, but patiently waited for my answer. The third time he asked me and I refused, he told me that he wouldn't ask me again.

Although Steven never raised the subject of marriage again, around the same time there were also some younger men who were interested in me. They came to me with various prophecies insisting that God had told them I was the right woman for them, but I always told them that, if that were the case, He would have told me too!

Prompted by these proposals, I began to think about – if I were to get married – what kind of man I would want to marry. Definitely a man who was passionate about God and knew God had called him to serve Him. Definitely a man I knew was in love with me. Definitely someone I knew as a friend and who would also be like a brother to me. As I compiled this list in my mind, I was shocked to discover that Steven perfectly fulfilled all the qualities I was looking for in a husband. He was passionate to serve God. He said he loved me. We had been good friends long before the subject of marriage had been raised. He was as close to me as a brother ... Suddenly I became aware that I had fallen in love with him without realizing it. What was I going to do now?

I was just about to go to Uganda to take a two-year course in "Clearing and Forwarding," to enable me to get a job in Customs and I knew I could not go without telling him how I felt. But now I was afraid that he might have changed his mind and I was going to make myself look really stupid. I went to see him in his office at the church. I sat down in the chair opposite him and asked, "Do you still have those silly ideas you told me about?"

"What silly ideas?" he asked ingenuously.

"Oh God, I'm going to look so stupid," I thought to myself. Speaking out loud, I said, "Those silly ideas about wanting to marry me."

"Yes, I do," he replied.

"Why do you think you should marry me?" I questioned, as if it were some sort of interview.

"Because I love you," he said, as well as many other wonderful things.

Before confessing my change of heart, I still had a number of questions I desperately needed him to answer. "Are you ready to marry a wife who has never had a family and does not have one now to support her in any way? Are you ready to face all the difficulties that will surely come because I have not received any real parenting to prepare me for marriage and tell me what it means to be in a relationship? I have been through such a lot, and I have always kept myself to myself. Are you ready to accept all the difficulties that I may give you because of what I have been through?"

With tears in his eyes, Steven replied, "I'm ready."

Then I said, "I have accepted you because I love you too."

We immediately became engaged, without a ring of course! It was 7 August 2000.

Even though I was now completely certain that I was in love with Steven and wanted to marry him, I did not want to rush into marriage, and neither did he – he was keen to see the church better established first. So off I went to Uganda for two years to study. When I finished the course in 2002, I came back to Rwanda and found a job. Steven and I were married on 1 March 2003.

Chapter 12

Two Miracle Babies

As soon as I was married I wanted to have a baby. Although no one could ever replace the family I had lost, I couldn't wait for Steven and I to begin to establish a family of our own. I was so excited when in April 2003 I discovered I was pregnant. As we dreamed together about our family, Steven and I decided that we would name our first son "Maxwell."

Only a couple of weeks after I had discovered I was pregnant, I started to bleed and, very anxious, I went to the doctor. He prescribed some tablets for me, which I took according to the prescription. A few days later, the bleeding increased and I began to experience severe pain in my womb. By now I was extremely worried and I went back to the doctor. When I got to the surgery, there was a long queue of people waiting and I did not manage to see him. I went back the next day to find an equally long queue of people but this time I knew I had to wait.

When I eventually saw the doctor, he was shocked to discover that I had taken all the tablets he had prescribed, saying that they should have been taken over a three-month period. It was clear that there had been a mistake with the

prescription. I was devastated when, after examining me, he
told me that I had lost the baby and would need a D and C. He
sent me home and told me to come back a few days later. The
agony was prolonged when, a week after the procedure, I
developed an infection and was told that, since the D and C
had not been carried out properly, it would have to be
done again.

I was heartbroken over the loss of our baby and cried and
cried. Steven tried to console me as best he could, promising
me that God would give us another baby. The loss of my
baby, devastating as it was in itself, was also touching into the
chasm of grief and loss in my life. I had lost my family and
now it seemed that I was also losing my hope of a future
family. Day after day I lay on my bed and cried. Was this same
cycle going to be repeated over and over again in my life? One
day, as I lay on my bed crying my heart out, I heard God
speaking to me. He promised me that before 2003 was at an
end I would be pregnant again. Believing that God had truly
spoken to me I let go of my sorrow and trusted Him to keep
His promise. Together Steven and I forgave the doctor whose
mistake had led to us losing the baby and began to believe
God for another baby. We were trusting God for another
Maxwell.

Three months later I became pregnant again. It was just
before Steven was leaving on an extended trip abroad and,
literally hours before his flight was due to depart, we managed
to fit in an appointment with a doctor – a different one this
time. To our great shock, the doctor informed me that I was
not pregnant but had a tumor in my womb. I refused to
believe what he was saying: I was convinced I was pregnant.
As Steven and I made our way home, feeling extremely
confused and upset, I stopped off at a supermarket and bought
a one-year-old child's shoe as a sign of my faith that my baby

would live. At the time all the money we had in the world was 5,000 Rwandan Francs (about £5) and I had used half of it to buy the shoe. Knowing that was all the money he had to leave with me, Steven was furious, but I told him that I felt I needed to buy it as a sign of my faith. "You could have waited a week or two till we had more money," he retorted. On the inside I was reeling from what the doctor had said and I knew I had to take a stand and believe God's promise.

On the way home from taking Steven to the airport, I began to feel very unwell and for the whole of the next week I was vomiting. By the end of the week I was vomiting blood and was aware that I had internal bleeding, and I knew I had to go back to the doctor. Still maintaining that I had a tumor, he sent me to have a scan. I had no confidence that the machine they were using was working properly and immediately decided to find another doctor who would give me a proper scan. When I made the appointment I simply told the doctor that I had been sick and wanted to check how my baby was doing. After examining me and carrying out the scan, he told me that I was three weeks' pregnant. I felt ecstatic. All the way home on the bus I was singing to myself with joy. When I reached home, I thanked God for my baby.

Four days later I became very sick again and started vomiting blood again. A close friend of ours, Martin, who works alongside Steven as an executive pastor at our church, took me to King Faysal Hospital in Kigali, where they diagnosed that I was suffering from ulcers. I was put on a drip and remained in hospital for two weeks. I had only been back at home for a week when the symptoms started up all over again. The doctor prescribed more medication and I was instructed not to get out of bed. My cousin Adeline came to stay with me and my Auntie Anita, who lives in Kigali, frequently came over to help.

The Bible tells us that there is an evil power at work on the earth, which it refers to as the devil, and throughout this time I knew that the devil was out to destroy my family. He had succeeded once, but I was determined that he was not going to succeed again. As I lay in my bed, feeling very, very weak, I constantly prayed that God would protect my family, often declaring to the devil that my son will live and not die. I visualized Maxwell putting on the "shoe of faith" and playing around in our home. Steven kept in close contact from the UK, ready to return home if I wanted him to.

As the days went on, my health continued to deteriorate and I was re-admitted into hospital. I took my little shoe with me. The medication no longer seemed to be having any effect. I was told I had an infection from my esophagus right down into my stomach and I was put back on a drip straightaway. I could not eat; all I could do was suck cubes of ice. I remained in the hospital for almost three months – all this time Steven was abroad.

I may have been desperately weak physically but spiritually I had never been stronger. I lay on my bed clutching my little shoe and telling the devil that he was not going to have my son. The worse my health became, the more my faith increased. Martin came to see me every day and I was always encouraged by his visit. Either Auntie Anita or my cousin Adeline or my best friend Julienne took it in turns to stay the night with me at the hospital.

Towards the end of the three months I started to feel a little better, although still incredibly weak, so the medical staff decided to send me home. It was a mistake. After two days I was so ill that Adeline and Geoffrey, one of Steven's friends, had to take me back to the hospital. The hospital refused to admit me until I had paid an advance on the cost of my care. They were demanding 60,000 Francs (£60) and, since I didn't have enough cash with me, I was left sitting in a chair in reception while Geoffrey went to fetch some more money. I felt absolutely terrible. I was still constantly vomiting blood and felt so weak that I thought I would pass out. Adeline was terrified that I was going to die sitting there in the chair.

The situation was saved by a nurse who happened to be walking through the reception area. She asked Adeline what was going on and when she realized why I was having to wait there, she was furious. Scolding the receptionist for leaving someone who was obviously so ill waiting there, she immediately called for a wheelchair. Once on the ward I was put straight back on the drip. I was so weak that I could not even lift my head to be sick, so everything came out of the side of my mouth.

Later on I lost consciousness. I was aware of people moving around the bed but I couldn't hear what they were saying. As I sank deeper and deeper into unconsciousness, I had a vision in which I saw myself lying in a coffin and Steven standing next to it crying. The spirit of death was very near. Then suddenly a voice broke into my unconsciousness. The voice clearly said, "You will not die but live, and declare the goodness of the Lord." As I woke up out of my unconscious state, I realized that a sheet had been placed over my face. When I removed it I saw Martin standing by my bed, crying and praying. I thought it was he who had spoken out the words I had heard but he told me he did not say them. "I will not die," I said out loud. At the sound of my voice Julienne, who had been sitting in a chair by my bed crying, burst out into fresh tears and Adeline and Auntie Anita, who had been crying outside the room, rushed in. Seeing how much they loved me, I cried too. Later that day Steven phoned. I was too exhausted to speak to

him but he spoke to Julienne, and she told me that he would
be home the next week.

Four months later I was lying in a bed in Dudley Road City
Hospital, Birmingham, holding Maxwell in my arms. Having
suffered so much trauma at the hands of medical practitioners
in Rwanda, Steven had decided that I must come to the
UK for the birth of our baby, even though it meant finding
a large sum of money. I arrived alone on a damp, dark
February day to stay in a country I had never visited before.
Fortunately some friends of mine from Rwanda called
Christel and Hassina had come to England to study and were
living at the home of another Rwandan called Viviane. They
welcomed me into their home and gave me a great deal of
support.

Steven arrived in time for my birthday in March and
together we waited for our baby's birth in May, two weeks
later than the due date we had been expecting. It was touch
and go as far as my visa was concerned. We were so grateful
for the excellent medical care I received in the hospital. People
in Britain may complain about their National Health Service,
but it is light years ahead of what I had experienced through
my recent illness. I was amazed to be asked such questions as,
"Is there anything you need?" or "Would you like a cup of
tea?" It was a far cry from a Rwandan hospital where you are
expected to sit quietly and wait for your turn to be delivered
and where it is quite common to be told, "Be quiet! Do you
think you're the first woman ever to give birth?"

For Steven too, it was a very different experience as in
Africa men are seldom present at the birth of their child and he
had never even witnessed a birth on the TV. We often laugh
as we look back since, concerned about the pain I was

experiencing, he kept saying, "Frida, I don't ever want to put you through this suffering again."

Packed in my hospital bag was the little shoe I had bought as a sign of my faith. As I held Maxwell in my arms, I placed the shoe on his tiny foot and looked up to heaven with joy, thanking God for the fulfillment of His promise in my life.

Fifteen months later, on Sunday 18 September 2005, we had just finished lunch when Steven received a phone call. It was from a man who lived next-door to the church, saying that his housegirl had just found an abandoned baby near the outside toilets. Since the baby had been left at the church, he was asking us to take responsibility for her. As that afternoon I was due to attend one of the local Gacaca meetings being held to try and bring reconciliation to the Rwandan people after the genocide, Steven rushed down to the church to see what could be done. He found the little baby where she had been abandoned on a little mat near the toilet. She was extremely dirty but nevertheless very beautiful. She seemed to be about three to four months old.

Steven immediately phoned me to ask me if he could bring the baby to me at the meeting but I told him that I would go straight home. I phoned Vicky and Giselle, who live with us, to warn them what was happening and made my way home to get things ready. The girls were shocked that any mother could abandon her baby like that, but they were excited about seeing her.

I was most concerned about how fifteen-month-old Maxwell would react to a new baby coming into the home and I wanted to prepare him. He was used to having all my attention and I didn't want him to feel pushed out. I sat him on my knees and explained to him about his new little sister. I reassured him that having another little baby around did not mean that I loved him any less but that he would be as important to me as he had always been. Of course, he didn't understand what I was saying but I felt it was very important for me to say it. Then I let him help me get out the little clothes he had worn when he was small.

An hour or so later Steven arrived back accompanied by our church neighbor's housegirl who was carrying the baby. We all crowded round excitedly to get our first glimpse and we all immediately fell in love with her. As I held her for the first time, even though she was extremely smelly and dirty, all I could see was a beautiful baby.

The first thing I did was to take her into Maxwell's bedroom to give her a bath. I don't think she had ever been bathed before. There were creatures crawling in her head; her nails which had been left to grow very long were black. Instead of a nappy she was wearing a piece of cloth with a plastic bag wrapped over it, and it looked as if she had been wearing it for days and days. I bathed her very carefully and then cut her nails. Once she had been washed I called Maxwell to come and help me dress her. As we did so, he kept saying "Baby, baby" and bending over to kiss her gently on the check. He did not seem jealous at all. Her old clothes I threw away apart from one item which I kept to show her when she was older.

When we rejoined the rest of the family in the living room we talked about what the new addition to the family should be called. I wanted to call her "Treasure" but Steven reminded me that we had agreed that if we ever had a daughter we would call her "Natasha." He then suggested that I gave her a middle name. Extremely grateful that we had found the baby alive, I decided that it should be *Ishimwe* which means "Thank God." To this day we have no idea who left

Natasha at the church nor any of the circumstances surrounding her birth. That first night little Natasha did not sleep very well. Each time she woke I picked her up and, lying her on my chest, whispered to her that she was now my daughter and that she was in a family where she would always be loved and where she would always be special.

Almost immediately I resigned from my job as Marketing Manager with a firm called Connectus, which represented other countries' interests in Rwanda, because I felt I needed to spend as much time with the two children as I could. We felt the loss of the income but we knew that the children were our priority. As Natasha settled she became a happy and contented child. Initially she had a few health problems and we had to take her to the hospital for regular appointments, but they soon cleared up. We informed the authorities of our desire to adopt her as our daughter and the legal formalities proceeded smoothly.

Soon after Natasha's arrival I bumped into my uncle in the town and told him that I had a new baby. Surprised, he said, "I didn't know that you were pregnant." When I explained to him how Natasha had come to us, he declared, "I'm coming round to your house tomorrow, and if that baby is a Hutu, you'll have to take her to an orphanage."

"Don't tell me what to do in my own home," I rebutted strongly. "She is an innocent child and she is God's gift to my family."

Chapter 13

UMUHOZA

Ever since I had become a Christian the desire to reach out to the aching people of Rwanda had been growing within me. I knew that it was not an accident that my parents had given me the name *Umuhoza* but that somehow they had sensed that it was my destiny to be a comforter and counselor of the broken-hearted. Many people were already coming to me to ask for advice and counsel and I helped them as best as I could, but sometimes I felt out of my depth and I wanted to receive some counseling training. Many of them were young people who had survived the genocide and were desperate to know how to forgive the men who had killed their families. Steven was very supportive of my desire, and together we looked for the best way to make this happen. I knew that at the right time and in the right place God would find a way for me to do it.

In 2004 an American couple called Larry and Lorrie Russell, who lead Shepherds' Heart Ministry based in Colorado, USA, came to preach at the annual convention of Rwanda for Jesus Ministries. Discovering that they both had degrees in counseling, I told them about my dream to do a course in counseling and they talked it through with me at length. When they left they promised that they would ask around to see if they could connect me with a college in the USA.

Because Maxwell was still so young (Natasha had not yet joined our family), at this stage the ideal solution as far as I could see was to try and find a course online. I spent hours at the Internet café trying to see what was available but I couldn't find anything. I turned my sights towards America but it soon became clear that the cost was prohibitive.

One day, while Steven was away on a trip in the USA, I was excited to discover that Hillsong in Australia ran a course in marriage counseling and the fees seemed reasonable. I printed out the prospectus and couldn't wait to show Steven when he arrived home. After discussing and praying about it together we agreed that I should apply for the course. We planned that I would take Maxwell with me. It would be a huge sacrifice to live apart for such a long period but we felt it would be worth it. I enrolled on the course and paid a deposit of $150, and was accepted. I was very excited about the amazing opportunity that was opening before me, but as I looked into it more and more I discovered that the cost of living in Australia was very high and I began to realize that it wasn't going to work. I would have to get a job to pay my way and I had no idea how I would organize care for Maxwell. I applied to Hillsong for a scholarship but my hopes were dashed when we discovered that the college did not offer scholarships. I was disappointed but determined not to give up.

Not long afterwards Steven was talking to a good friend of his from London, Pastor Kofi Banful and happened to mention to him that I was really wanting to do a counseling course. He suggested that I try South Africa and offered to sponsor me to do the course. I was thrilled! South Africa seemed ideal as it was so much closer to home, but my search for a course at a university there proved fruitless. Hearing this, Pastor Kofi suggested that he could speak to a friend of his, Dr Femi, who was Principal of South London Bible College, England. On doing so he discovered that the college, which had an impressive record, offered a two-year counseling diploma. The diploma itself was not the important thing for me, as it was the training I was really looking for, but it was an added bonus.

Dr Femi offered me a one-year scholarship at a new branch of the college in Luton and I leapt at it! The course was due to begin in January 2006. Pastor Kofi offered to pay for my second year. I immediately started to make arrangements to travel to the UK and went to apply for a visa. The offer of a scholarship made everything very straight-forward. Just at that time an Australian called Rob came to stay with us for a few days. When he heard about my plans, he offered to pay for my flight to the UK, which we took as confirmation from God that I was headed in the right direction. Days later I was sitting on a plane bound for England. Although it was not easy for me to leave my family – especially as Natasha had only recently arrived – I knew I had to go ahead.

On 4 January I arrived in the UK, ready to start my course a week later. I was staying with my Rwandan friends Christel and Hassina, who by this time were living in Solihull. The first time I went down to Luton to register at the college it was a complete disaster. I had gone with a friend who was working as a lecturer in one of the colleges in Luton. When we found the address I had for the college, we discovered it had moved, and when we got to the new address, there was no one there. It was a completely wasted trip. I returned home very frustrated and disappointed. We set off again the following Tuesday, 10 January, the day my course was due to start. A much bigger disappointment was awaiting me. I had not interpreted the course prospectus correctly and so, when I arrived to register, I discovered that the course I was proposing to attend only had two hours a month assigned to counseling – and, in fact, it had started the previous September. Not only was the counseling content of the course minimal, I had missed a whole term! Furthermore, in order to fulfill the terms of my visa, which required that I study for at least twenty-two hours a week, I would have to fill the rest of my time with other courses such as theology and music, but I was very clear in my mind why I had come all this way – I wanted to get some training in counseling. It was a huge dilemma and I felt very homesick.

As well as the confusion over the course, I was finding living in England and commuting between Birmingham and Luton very expensive. The money I had brought with me was disappearing fast. I felt very confused about what to do. It seemed such a waste to spend two years away from my family for just two hours' counseling training a month.

It was in the midst of my sense of confusion and uncertainty that James and Tina Stacey, friends of Steven's, invited me to spend a night at their home. James and Steven had originally met at a convention with Lift Up Jesus Global Ministries in Kabale, Uganda, in 2002. During the evening I was able to talk about the problems I was experiencing regarding the course. It was such a relief to be able to open up to someone about it. As we chatted, James and Tina told me about Ellel Ministries International which has a worldwide reputation for its counseling training and ministry. A couple called Ray and Christa Eicher, whom Tina had worked with in India with Operation Mobilisation many years ago, were now leaders of Ellel India.

Together we looked at the Ellel Ministries' website and saw that there was a one-week Restoration course starting on 8 February which seemed tailor-made. I was overwhelmed when Tina and James offered to pay for me to attend the course. After the Restoration Week there was a possibility of going on a nine-week Flagship training course at Ellel's Headquarters, near Lancaster. Instead of being away from home on a long drawn-out two-year course, I would be able to finish my training by early July 2006 and then return to my family – a much better arrangement. I began to feel excited again. As well as a sense of being back on the right track, it was such a relief not to have to be away from my family for so long, which I knew was not ideal with the children at such a young age.

I was even more overjoyed when, the following morning, James and Tina invited me to come and stay with them until the course began. Knowing that they were very tired, after having nursed Tina's father until he had died a few months earlier, I was very touched by their warmth and hospitality. They welcomed me like a daughter and made me feel very much at home.

Having explained my change of plan to Pastor Kofi, South London Bible College and the Home Office, I began to look forward to the Restoration Week at Glyndley Manor. From the moment I arrived I loved the place and all the people from all over the world whom I met there. The teaching on the course impressed me from the outset and I knew without a shadow of a doubt that I was in the right place. God showed me very early on that before I could minister to other people I needed to receive healing first. Through the teaching I came to discover that my emotions were locked up deep inside me and they needed sorting out.

Since becoming a Christian the Spirit of God had helped

me to control them, but they were still there buried deep within and they were stopping me becoming the person God intended me to be. Because I had wanted to be strong so that I could help others, I had developed a hard exterior, as though nothing affected me. Reflecting upon the truth that God was showing me I realized that this hard exterior was affecting all my relationships, stopping me giving myself fully to those closest to me. As God spoke to me through the lectures and seminars I began to realize just how much grief there was still locked up inside me, which He wanted me to start letting out. I began to understand that I had never grieved properly. God was showing me that it was now time to grieve. It was now time to grieve the brutal murder of my most precious family and the life that we should have enjoyed together.

As I held back, fearing that grieving would negate the process of forgiving my family's killers which had cost me so dear, God reassured me that crying and grieving did not mean that I had not forgiven. Crying and grieving was a proper response to deep loss. The Holy Spirit began to open the door in my heart which I had slammed firmly shut in the early days after the genocide. I cried many, many tears that week. The tears flowed in my times of prayer on my own and in the prayer times I had with trained counselors available to help those on the course. As the tears poured out, I began to find great healing and release. The tears had been locked up inside me all these many years and now – at last – I was able to let them go. I felt a great sense of relief. My healing had begun, but I was very aware there was still a long way to go.

I knew that it was going to be very important for me to be able to do Ellel's nine-week course but had no idea how I was going to be able to find the money. It was only through

James and Tina's generosity that I had been able to do the Restoration Week. I knew that I would have to rely on God, who had already provided for me in so many wonderful ways. Before the week ended God had begun to answer my prayer. One of the couples on the course, whom I had really come to love and appreciate, told me that they were going to send a cheque for £800 to Ellel as a contribution towards my fees if I was able to do the course. If I was not able to take it up, it would be made available to someone else. Their wonderful gift came completely out of the blue as I hadn't told anyone that I needed money to do the course. God's provision was amazing. Encouraged, I kept praying, "God, you know how much I want to do this course – and not just for me, but for others too. Please make it possible." The £800 was a start, but there was still over £1,000 to find.

I left Glyndley Manor overjoyed at all that God was doing in my life but aware that there was unfinished business. I couldn't wait to tell James and Tina, who had just been away on a much-needed holiday break in Madeira, about all that had happened – about all the wonderful people I had met and the deep healing that was going on in my life.

Amidst the joy and excitement of all that was happening, there was one rather large disappointment. Steven had been planning to come and see me, bringing Maxwell with him – we had agreed it would be too difficult for him to manage on his own with two young children and it would be better for Natasha to stay at home with Vicky, who came to live with us when Maxwell was born to help me look after him, having previously lived in a very difficult situation. Steven had been hoping to surprise me for my birthday in March, but Maxwell had been refused a visa – the Home Office took the view that since I was studying in the UK, there was a high chance that once my son was in the country, we might request asylum.

Having been looking forward to seeing them both so much, I could not hide my disappointment. That evening James and Tina told me that they wanted to pay for me to go home and see my family before I went on the NETS school. Once again I was overwhelmed by their love and generosity. Naturally I would have loved to take them up on their kind offer, but it didn't seem right to travel all that way when I didn't have the money for the course yet. I explained why I was hesitating and they replied, "We can pray about that." I resolved to spend the next morning praying and fasting.

The next morning God stepped in again in a miraculous way. As I was praying I heard James call up to me, telling me that I had a phone call. I told him I was praying and couldn't come to the phone, but the person on the other end of the phone was fairly insistent. It was Constance Funck, who had become a very close friend during the Restoration Week. After telling her that Maxwell had been refused a visa and, therefore, Steven and he were no longer coming to visit, she said, "Do you still have it in mind to do the nine-week school?" When I said that I was still hoping that God would make it possible, she astounded me by saying, "Well, I didn't want to say anything while you were still on the Restoration Week, but my husband and I believe that God has been telling us to pay for you to do the school. Now you can go home and see your family."

I couldn't believe what I was hearing. When I told Constance that someone else had already offered to pay £800 towards the fees, she simply said I could use the rest of the money for living expenses. I thanked her from the bottom of my heart and then, as soon as I put the phone down, I shouted out, "James! Tina!" and burst into tears. "James! Tina! I'm going on the course! I'm going on the course!"

James appeared and, seeing me crying, asked, "Frida! What is it? What's the problem?"

"There are no problems," I said, "there are only answers!", as I told him about the amazing conversation I had just had with Constance. God was doing so much more for me than I could ever have expected. Not only was He making it possible for me to go on the NETS school, but He was allowing me to go home for a visit!

My trip back home to Rwanda flew by. It was wonderful to be able to reassure myself that the children were well and also to be able to tell Steven all about the deep work of healing God was accomplishing in my life. It was the breather I needed to enable me to return to England ready to make the most of the intensive nine weeks ahead. I wanted to learn as much as I could about the important subjects covered during the school, such as finding healing after trauma and serious accident, and other related topics.

As with the first course, right from its beginning the Flagship school seemed tailored specifically for me. Every subject covered in the lectures seemed to touch into an area in my life. Almost every day I phoned Steven full of excitement to tell him about what God had been showing me and the areas of my life He had been touching into. I don't know how many times Steven wished that he could have been there on the course with me.

When we were well into the school, all the students were asked to write down details of any major traumas they had had so that people could be prayed for during the course. Some of them were selected to be prayed for by Ellel's founder and International Director, Peter Horrobin. I really hoped that I would be chosen, and Steven and I prayed together over the phone about this. I was thrilled when I heard that I had been.

God had already been doing so much in my life but the opportunity to be prayed for with Peter seemed to help me leap over the final obstacle on my journey. Peter listened very carefully as I told him my story and then he invited the Holy Spirit to come as we prayed together. He prayed about a number of areas but as one very specific prayer he asked God to heal the injury I had sustained to the back of my neck when the killers had attempted to murder me. Over the years I had continued to suffer head and back pain as a result of the injury which flared up from time to time, and Steven had always intended that, when we could, we would see a specialist at a western hospital about it. I had had another bout of pain while I was at the school and in fact the whole week before that time of prayer I had a terrible headache. Ever since the genocide I had also continued to suffer from very frightening nightmares from time to time. As Peter prayed for God to take away the consequences of the terrible traumas I had gone through and to heal my broken heart the headache vanished, and from that time to this I have never had it again. The nightmares also ceased.

I had thought I was whole when I became a Christian. Then God had showed me that I needed to forgive. I had thought I was whole when I had forgiven, but God had showed me that wholeness would come as I released to Him all the pain and grief I had locked up inside me. I understood that the healing of my head wound was in fact a sign that all my inner pain and trauma was gone – forever taken away as Jesus carried it on my behalf on the cross. I had been looking for a counseling course to fill my head, but now I understood that it was my heart that needed to be filled. Only with a full heart could I impact other people's broken lives. Now I was ready to fulfill my destiny as Umuhoza – to bring God's powerful healing to the broken-hearted.

Chapter 14

DESTINED TO LIVE

It has been thirteen years now since the genocide took place but every time I talk about it, it is as if it just happened yesterday. I don't know whether that will ever change, but my traumatic memories now have no power over me. That is not to say that I do not still feel the acute loss of my family, but the past no longer holds me back. Although my enemies chose me to die, I know that God destined me to live! I know that there was a very special reason why I lived and fifteen members of my family died, and I am determined to fulfill the destiny that God has for my life. Indeed, some of that destiny I have already fulfilled, but I know there is more to come – much more!

In terms of the genocide's impact on my family there remains for me one very real sadness, and that is that I have not as yet been able to locate my father's body and give him a proper and honorable burial. It is an ongoing search, but one that I will not give up until I have exhausted every avenue.

When I returned home from Gabon as a sixteen-year-old, I was heart-broken to discover that in my absence my Uncle Emile had exhumed the bodies of my family and reburied them in a communal grave next to my grandfather's house. The grave contains fifteen bodies – it should have contained sixteen! I know that the reason he did it in my absence was to spare me further pain, but unwittingly he robbed me of an appropriate and necessary part of the grieving process. To tell the truth, not being there on that occasion broke my heart even more. I am, however, extremely grateful that my beloved family is buried together in a place where they will always be remembered. In fact, just across the track from the grave, there is a mass grave containing the remains of 1,200 Tutsis, which is in the process of being made into a public memorial site for the citizens of Nyanza. The authorities chose to position it near my grandfather's house because he was such a respected and revered member of the community. I would dearly love to be able to contribute in some way to its completion.

Despite my continued efforts, the search for my father's body has as yet proved fruitless. My main hope in locating it lies with his killer, François, but since that day when I visited him in prison to tell him I had forgiven him, on which occasion he freely admitted to having murdered my father, François has changed his tune.

As soon as I heard that François had been released from prison, I felt compelled to go and see him again. My only reason for going was to beg him to tell me where my father's body is buried. It was 27 September 2006 and, even though it was raining that day, I still decided to go because I was desperate to hear what he had to say. I really wanted to get to the truth.

My cousin Nepo came with me, and we stood and talked on the doorstep of François' house in the rain. To both Nepo's and my surprise François recognized my cousin but not me. As before, his attitude was hostile and defensive. He seemed to be looking down his nose at me as if to say, "What do you want?"

"Don't you know who this is?" Nepo asked. When it was clear that François didn't, Nepo continued, "Please try and remember your former neighbors – she is one of their daughters. Surely you can remember?"

Seeing that Nepo was beginning to get upset, I broke in and said, "I know it's been a while since you saw me, but I am Frida, Bernard's daughter. I have come to ask you some important things that I want to know about my father."

Before I had even finished my sentence, François said aggressively, "And do you think I know? I don't know anything about your father at all ... at all."

When he said that, I was really taken aback. By this point in the conversation it had begun to rain much harder and his wife and children, who were just returning to the house, urged us to come inside, but we stayed where we were. Feeling desperate to get hold of the one piece of information I had come to discover, I pressed François, saying, "Please ... You're the one who told me that you had killed my father when I came to see you in 1999. Now you're denying it, but that's OK. At least, if you know where the body is, please show me. I have not come to judge you, but to ask you please to help me."

"OK," he replied. "If that's all you want, let's go. I'm sure that his body was taken to be buried with the rest of your family but, anyway, let's go."

When we reached the stretch of road where the roadblock had been set up during the genocide and used as a killing center, François stopped. "This is the place," he said. "Bernard came up from his father's house and found me sitting here by the roadblock. He looked absolutely terrified. He wasn't wearing shoes but was just in his socks. He told me that he wanted to die because he had just seen his wife and children being killed and he couldn't face going on living. I told him to leave but he wouldn't listen to me. In fact, he seemed very confused. He asked me to kill him, but I insisted that I couldn't do such a thing. So he said he was going to wait for the killers to come back from his father's home, knowing that they would kill him. I begged him to leave but he wouldn't. Instead he sat down with his head between his knees and just waited. He was breathing very fast."

After a pause, he continued, "Not long afterwards the killers who'd gone to your grandfather's house came back and found him there. They asked me what he was doing there, but I told them that he was a brother and they should leave him alone. They ordered me to kill him but I refused. Just then your father said that he had some beers that he'd been keeping at Kabayiza's house since before all the killing had started and that he wanted us all to have a drink on him. So we all went to Kabayiza's house. When we got there, your father told Kabayiza to bring the beer and he did. While we were drinking together, your father told us that he'd given a cow to Kabayiza and that no one should take it away from him.

"Before we'd finished drinking the beers, some more of the killers who'd been at your grandfather's house came and discovered us all there. When they found me and your father sitting side by side, they were furious. 'How dare you sit there with that cockroach we've been searching for for a month now!' they shouted. I told them that he wasn't a cockroach but a brother, but they wouldn't listen. They told him to stand up and then they pushed him out telling him to go with them. Then we all came back here. When we got here, your father begged us to give him just a few minutes to pray, which they did and while he was praying, I stepped back."

"What did he say in his prayer?" I asked.

"I told you I stepped back because I didn't want to see him being killed, so I couldn't hear his prayer, but I did hear him say 'Amen' and, as soon as he said it, he was hit on the back of his head with a big stick. He didn't scream – he just died there and then."

"Who hit him?" I demanded to know. "Because if you were standing nearby, you know at least who did it, don't you?"

"Karori hit him," he replied.

By then I was so upset that I felt like crying, but I swallowed my tears because I didn't want him to see me crying and stop telling me his story. As he spoke, I was filming him and recording his voice using my mobile phone.

"I swear I didn't kill your father," François continued, "even if I confessed it in prison. I saw him being killed, but I didn't touch him."

"Are you sure you didn't do anything to my father?" I pressed. "That you just looked on while he was being killed? Why didn't you do something then?"

"Because I would have been putting my life at risk too. I'd tried to persuade him to get out of there and he refused – what else could I have done?" he said.

"Are you very sure that it was all done here?" I asked.

"Yes, I'm very sure. The reason I know that his body was buried with the others is because people told me," he added.

"How do you know?" Nepo interrupted angrily. "Now that you've told us what you know, just leave it to us and we'll do the rest." Trying to calm him down, I put my hand on his shoulder and said, "Nepo, it's OK. There's no need to be angry. What was done was done. Let's go now. I've seen the place and that's all I wanted. Let's go." Then, turning to François I took my farewell, saying, "Thank you very much for your time and for bearing with me in the rain. Please feel free to get in touch with me any time and tell me anything else that you remember. You can always tell my cousin Emmanuel who lives in this area and I can come back any time you want to talk to me. I want you to know that I have forgiven all of you with all my heart."

At that he just said, "No, there's nothing else to add to what I've told you. I've told you everything I know. Don't ask me ever again. I'm innocent. If I'd done it, I would have told you, and that's that."

Thanking him again, we took our leave.

I left feeling extremely upset that this man had changed his story. When I got home that evening, exhausted, I related the whole conversation to Steven and played him the recording I had made on my mobile phone. I knew François was lying to me because there were eye-witness accounts of him murdering my father. With Steven's support I decided to return to Nyanza the following Wednesday when François was due to appear before the Gacaca hearing.

The Gacaca (meaning "justice on the grass") is a process of local judgment in which the perpetrators of the genocide are brought before the community – in the village or town meeting place – and expected to tell the truth about their involvement. Realizing that, using the normal justice system, it would take at least a hundred years to try the enormous number of cases resulting from the genocide, the Government resorted to a modernized form of the traditional Gacaca system to seek to bring justice. At the Gacaca hearings survivors who suffered at the hands of the accused and eye-witnesses are also able to give their account of the events. Everyone is expected to tell the truth about what they have seen or experienced, and they are not allowed to speak about what they have heard second-hand. Anyone summoned to the Gacaca is required to attend – if they are out of the country for any reason, they must return for it.

François' denial of his previous confession is sadly not unusual. A couple of years ago, due to massive prison overcrowding, the Government declared that anyone who confessed their crimes would be freed. Many of the killers confessed, in order to get out of prison, only to recant their confession once they were released. For the victims of their crimes this is extremely painful and difficult. It is heartbreaking when the person you know without a shadow of a doubt is guilty of the crime denies it.

It is a two-hour drive from Kigali to Nyanza and then I had to take a motorbike-taxi to the place where the Gacaca was being held. By the time I arrived at the Gacaca it had already started. François was standing in front of all the people who had gathered, holding his hands to his chest. I don't think he had expected to see me ever again and that is why he had lied to me. When I walked in, he turned to look at me and as our eyes met, he immediately looked down. I kept my eyes fixed on him and, seconds later, he looked up again, met my gaze and turned away, swallowing hard. I don't think he had expected me to come all the way from Kigali to the Gacaca and realized that things were not going to go well for him.

I listened as a number of people came forward to testify that François had been among the killers who had gone to my grandfather's house on 7 May 1994, which he was denying. Addressing François directly, the official presiding over the Gacaca asked, "Did you go in that group, François?"

"No, I did not," he stated.

Then a woman called Donatilla rose to her feet. She had been married to my uncle and was one of my mother's close friends. Her husband and six children had been murdered by the same band of killers who had murdered my family. She addressed François directly: "François, you are denying going to Munyabitare's house that morning. If someone who

survived your killing spree can testify that you were there, will
you still deny it?"

François did not have an answer to her question. He looked
down and he appeared to be shaking. Of course, Donatilla had
been referring to me. I had not come to the Gacaca to try and
make François confess that he had been among the group of
killers who had murdered my family – I just wanted to hear
the truth about my father.

I stood up. First apologizing to the committee and the
assembled group of people that I had arrived late, I asked if it
was possible for François' statement to be read out again as I
had missed it. I felt sure it was going to be different from what
he had told me the previous week. Without hesitating, the
presiding official read it out again. In it François said he was
among the group of killers that had murdered my father. As
the statement was being read out François was nervously
shuffling from one foot to the other, looking very ashamed.
The official asked him whether there was something he
wanted to add. At this he said, "I witnessed the death of
Bernard and I beat him with a stick, but Karori finished him,
and I ask for forgiveness."

I continued: "You see, last time we spoke, you yourself
denied that you even approached my dad when he was being
killed, but now you are saying that you beat him with a stick!
What size was your stick, because I really think that my father
was too strong to be killed by a stick?"

"My stick wasn't big. But I didn't kill him, Karori did," he
insisted.

Then a woman called Josepha stood up. "You're lying," she
said angrily. "We have heard that you killed Bernard after you
killed his family. You even took his clothes and his shoes. And
I'm sure you were not alone. We can call your fellow killers to
come and testify against you. I'm a Hutu like you and I

followed all that went on in the genocide. I know you killed Bernard, so don't deny it. Look, you are breaking his daughter's heart – tell the truth so that she can bury her father. Because we all know that it's you who did it." With these words she sat down, looking very annoyed.

After her a soldier called Innocent got to his feet. He was my father's cousin and the person who had actually arrested François after the genocide. He said, "François, what has come over you? Why can't you make things easy for yourself and just tell the truth for once? You yourself told me what happened when I arrested you. You said you'd killed Bernard with a stick after he'd prayed. You told us that he'd given you beer and even that you'd demanded 5,000 Rwandan Francs from him, but when you discovered that he only had some dollars and his passport, you refused it, saying you wanted real money not paper, because you didn't even know what dollars were. You told me that you tore the dollars up and threw them on the floor. And now here you are, denying everything."

When Innocent had finished speaking, the presiding official of the Gacaca decided to call to the front a man who had been François' constant companion throughout the genocide. It was Gatoya, my grandfather's killer. Gatoya came forward, looking absolutely terrified. His eyes were darting here, there and everywhere as if he was looking for someone, and his hands were clasped tightly together. The presiding official asked him to raise his hand and swear to tell the truth in God's name. When Gatoya had done so, he asked him, "Tell the truth: you were with the group that went to Munyabitare's home and killed people there on the morning of 7 May 1994. Was François with you?"

Without hesitating Gatoya replied, "Yes, he was with us. All we did, we did together. I guess we can't have buried the bodies properly because I hear that Bernard's little girl survived."

"Would you recognize that girl if you saw her?" the presiding official asked.

"No, I don't think so, because it was dark, but I was told in prison that she is alive."

At that moment I stood up and said, "Gatoya, look at me. I'm the one that you buried alive. Do you know me now?"

"Yes, I know you," he replied.

Then I said, "All I want to know is about my dad, because I know everything else – after all, I was there. Please tell us."

Fear was written all over François' face. He swallowed hard once again and shifted his position. Then the presiding official asked Gatoya, "Can you tell us how many people François killed there?"

"No, I can't tell you how many he killed," Gatoya replied, "because we were all too busy killing. He's the one who can tell you, because he's the one who knows."

The presiding official continued, "Gatoya, can you tell us anything about Bernard's death?"

"Bernard's death? Ask François because he's the one who was responsible for it. I can't say anything because I didn't kill him – François did."

"Thank you," the presiding official said, dismissing Gatoya. "We wanted the truth and now we have it. You can go."

Next to be called was a man called Dismas. Dismas was François' nephew and he had also been among the group that had killed my family. He was a man with a lot of blood on his hands and, in particular, he had killed many babies. Nevertheless, people used to refer to him as a "man of truth" because he spoke the truth about what had happened and his part in it. When he came forward, people knew they were going to hear what had really happened. Once Dismas was sworn in, the presiding official put his first question: "Dismas, we all know that François is your uncle. Did he go with you to Munyabitare's home the morning his family were killed?"

"Yes, he was with us."

"How many people did you kill there?"

"I really can't say. There were a lot of people there, both old and young. We beat them and then we killed them. I can't say how many," Dismas declared.

"What do you know about Bernard's death?" the presiding official then asked.

"My Uncle François killed him. He knows all the details because he even confessed it in the statement he made."

With the corroborating testimony of these two fellow killers, everyone now knew without a shadow of doubt that François had killed my father. By this time it was very late and the presiding official of the court concluded the proceedings, saying that the final decision about François' case would be given the following Wednesday. I had to rush off home because it was already dark and I had a long way to go.

As I mulled over the day's events on my journey home, I could feel only pity for François. I saw how hard it was for him to tell the truth and prayed for him to be released to tell the truth so that he could find peace. Later that evening Steven and I prayed together for all the people who had been involved with the Gacaca proceedings that day.

When the Gacaca reassembled the following week, it was without François. He had disappeared, and to this day has not been brought to justice. The decision of the Gacaca, given in his absence, was that François should return to prison because he had not spoken the truth in the statement he had made and was regarded as a danger to society. For me and for many of the families of his other victims, it is very painful to live with the fact that he has neither been brought to justice nor has been forced to divulge the truth about the crimes.

Though I carry no bitterness in my heart towards the killers of my family, it is fundamentally right and proper to see justice carried out on those responsible for heinous acts of bloodshed. Furthermore, the freedom of these killers causes many survivors of the genocide to live in fear. In the rural areas of Rwanda many Tutsi survivors have been murdered in order to prevent them testifying against Hutu killers. It is a very worrying situation, causing many Tutsis to move into the cities where they feel safer.

And so, my search for my father's body continues. I pray that one day I will see his body laid to rest. Through later Gacaca trials I have come to discover that François killed my father naked, which puts his killing into the highest category of crimes, as it demonstrates that it was a premeditated and deliberate act.

I really thank God that He has enabled me to forgive because now I can live a free and happy life. Many people – including many survivors of the genocide – ask me why I choose to forgive my enemies. I tell them that Jesus forgave me, and therefore I must forgive. I wasn't worthy of His forgiveness, but He gave it freely anyway. And anyone who calls themselves a follower of Jesus Christ must do the same.

Rwanda is a country making good and positive strides forward. A visitor to our beautiful land will see a country whose economy is growing, with flourishing businesses, new houses being built, and a bright, new generation rising up full of hope and desiring a better way of life. You do not have to dig very far below the surface, however, to discover that my nation is still hurting very deeply.

In Rwanda 40 percent of the nation are under the age of fifteen. There are hundreds of thousands of orphans. As a result of the genocide women outnumber men by a long way. Thousands of women who were the victims of brutal and repeated rape during the genocide are now suffering from HIV/AIDS. There are many, many survivors of the genocide who have not found a way to come to terms with what happened and are still battling with trauma, loss and pain. A high proportion of these are young people who will carry the trauma they suffered in the formative years of their childhood through the rest of their lives.

After the genocide there were so many orphans that many, many people opened their homes to take them in, which was a wonderful thing, but it means that large numbers of these extended families, often headed by a woman on her own, live below the poverty line. In fact, even today in Rwanda, almost two-thirds of our population of almost 9 million live below the poverty line. Many orphaned children do not have the means to attend school. Many have turned to alcohol to dull their pain, and many young women have resorted to prostitution as a means of survival. I sometimes think that what I went through is nothing when compared to what these young people are continuing to suffer.

Each year the first seven days of April are set aside as a Week of Mourning for the genocide. Each year, as a result, the unhealed, raw wounds are exposed as television and radio programs revisit the events of the genocide, showing distressing footage of Tutsis being hunted down and killed by Hutus, of mutilated and murdered bodies tossed aside in toilets, latrine pits or left by the side of the road, and mass graves containing thousands of corpses. The aim is memorial but in my view, during this week, my country is overwhelmed by death once again. I do not think this is healthy, and for my part

I choose to spend the seven days fasting and praying for my country's healing. I fervently believe that prayer is the best gift I can give to my nation, for I know what it has been through and I couldn't bear for another generation to have to face the hatred we had to face. Prayer changes all things.

But prayer on its own is not enough: the suffering need help, and I know that God is calling me to play my part. When I needed help, God sent His servants to come alongside me and help me, and I want to do the same for others who are suffering the same distress that I was suffering. I know that God heals the broken-hearted. In chapter 13 I told of my calling to be a counselor and comforter to my people and the beginning steps I have made to train myself to make me effective in this role. In future years, as my family responsibilities make it possible, I hope to undergo further training.

I also have a great desire to bring help to some of the many orphans of Rwanda. Steven and I already have an extended family. As well as our two children, Maxwell and Natasha, we have five young people living with us: Steven's sister Jessica, who is fifteen and has lived with us since she was four; Giselle, an orphan, who is sixteen and has lived with us since she was thirteen; Adeline, my cousin, who is the same age as me and lost her parents, four brothers and three sisters in the genocide; Vicky, also a survivor of the genocide, who has lived with us since the children were born; and, last but not least, the most recent addition, Bosco, who was added to our family when Steven refused to send him away after he came to our house with nowhere else to go. Each of these young people has been through so much, but with our support they are all getting their lives back together again. They are each very special to us.

My dream in the future is to be able to use a large plot of land which my father owned in Kigali to build a village where orphans can be cared for in small family units. This dream will only come to fruition if God provides the resources, but I believe He will.

I love my family so much. I thank God that He has provided me with a wonderful husband, who loves me with all his heart, and two beautiful children, soon to be three. They fill the gap that my family left but I never stop missing them. I always wish that my family, especially Mama, could see my family. I wish I could show her that all her discipline and strictness made me what I am today and enabled me to carry on and make something out of my life. But I hope to meet them all in heaven: Mama and Papa, my brothers Kiki, Alestide and Régis, my sisters Mimi and Gatesi, and my grandfather and grandmother. I am looking forward to that reunion ... and, best of all, meeting Jesus, my Strong Deliverer and Savior.

> Then I saw a new heaven and a new earth, for the first heaven and the first earth had passed away ... And I heard a loud voice from the throne saying, "Now the dwelling of God is with men, and he will live with them. They will be his people, and God himself will be with them and be their God. He will wipe every tear from their eyes. There will be no more death or mourning or crying or pain, for the old order of things has passed away." He who was seated on the throne said, "I am making everything new!"
>
> (Revelation 21:1, 3–4)

Sovereign World Ltd
&
Ellel Ministries International

In a stroke of divine master planning both Sovereign World and Ellel Ministries were independently founded in the same year – 1986.

Sovereign World, founded by Chris Mungeam, has become a widely respected Christian publishing imprint and Ellel Ministries, founded by Peter Horrobin, has developed a world-wide network of Centres, each designed to resource and equip the Church through healing retreats, courses and training schools.

Twenty years later, in April 2006, Ellel Ministries purchased Sovereign World Ltd to continue the precious work of publishing outstanding Christian teaching, as well as to create a publishing arm for Ellel Ministries. It was a divine knitting together of these two organizations both of which share the vision to proclaim the Kingdom of God by preaching the good news, healing the broken-hearted and setting the captives free.

If you would like to know more about Ellel Ministries their UK contact information is:

International Headquarters
Ellel Grange
Ellel
Lancaster
LA2 0HN
UK

Tel: +44 (0)1524 751651
Fax: +44 (0)1524 751738
Email: info@grange.ellel.org.uk

For details of other Centres please refer to the website at:
www.ellelministries.org

Today in one of Southern Africa's most disaster-torn nations, Rolland and Heidi Baker are at the center of a major move of God's Spirit. The last four years have seen them plant and take responsibility for around 6,000 churches as thousands of Mozambiquans have given their lives to Christ in an unprecedented revival. During this time they have also witnessed numerous acts of God's power. Miracles of provision, healing, deliverance, and even raising the dead, have followed. This is their amazing story.

There is Always Enough *by Rolland & Heidi Baker*
£8.99 | 978-185240-2877 | 192pp | Sovereign World Ltd

visions beyond
THE VEIL
GOD'S REVELATION TO CHILDREN OF HEAVEN AND HELL

H.a.BaKeR

FOREWORD BY ROLLAND AND HEIDI BAKER

Originally published many years ago, this outstanding
book is fresh and challenging to us today. It tells the
story of a group of children – mostly street beggars
or orphans – living in the Adullam Rescue Mission in
Yunnan Province, China, under the care of mission-
aries H.A. Baker and his wife. These children came
under an immense outpouring of the Holy Spirit – so
much so that they experienced visions of heaven, were
aware of angels, and were able to describe in great
detail what they saw. Challenging, thought-provoking
and faith-lifting.

Visions Beyond the Veil *by H.A. Baker*
£5.99 | 978-185240-4574 | 96pp | Sovereign World Ltd